BHAGMATI

AF646982

BHAGMATI

Why Hyderabad's Lost Queen Is the Soul of the City

MOUPIA BASU

Published by Westland Non-Fiction, an imprint of Westland Books, a division of Nasadiya Technologies Private Limited, in 2024

No. 269/2B, First Floor, 'Irai Arul', Vimalraj Street, Nethaji Nagar, Alapakkam Main Road, Maduravoyal, Chennai 600095

Westland, the Westland logo, Westland Non-Fiction and the Westland Non-Fiction logo are the trademarks of Nasadiya Technologies Private Limited, or its affiliates.

Copyright © Moupia Basu, 2024

Moupia Basu asserts the moral right to be identified as the author of this work.

ISBN: 9789360452872

10 9 8 7 6 5 4 3 2 1

The views and opinions expressed in this work are the author's own and the facts are as reported by her, and the publisher is in no way liable for the same.

All rights reserved

Typeset by Ashutosh Jha

Printed at Parksons Graphics Pvt. Ltd

No part of this book may be reproduced, or stored in a retrieval system, or transmitted in any form or by any means, electronic, mechanical, photocopying, recording, or otherwise, without express written permission of the publisher.

I dedicate this book to the people of Hyderabad.

Contents

Preface

In the old city of Hyderabad, there is a four hundred-and-forty-six-year-old bridge called the Purana Pul (old bridge). Constructed in 1578 by Ibrahim Qutb Shah,[1] the six hundred feet long and thirty-six feet wide bridge stands fifty-four feet above the riverbed and has twenty-two arches. This bridge, the first to be constructed in the area that later became Hyderabad, survived even the great Musi flood of 1908. However, by the middle to late twentieth century, it was dilapidated and crumbling, in need of urgent repair.

A little more than two decades ago, on World Tourism Day in September 2002, construction workers swarmed the Purana Pul to restore it to its former glory. When it was safe for use again, G. Kishan Rao, director of the then Andhra Pradesh tourism department, hit upon an idea to raise local awareness about the newly repaired bridge. Drawing on the origin story of the Purana Pul, he organised a lovers' day or couples' day on the bridge. The idea was a grand success. Hyderabadis thronged the area and, for a while, the Purana Pul was even called the Pyarana Pul (lovers' bridge).

The new name did not last long, but perhaps it should be restored. The way Hyderabadis turned out for the event showed that the story behind the origins of the Purana Pul remains as cherished in the hearts of the city's newest generations as it was nearly five centuries ago when the bridge was under construction. This story is one Hyderabadis love to tell over and over again, one that resides in their hearts, one they choose to believe even though there is no historical evidence of its existence. It is the story of a love so powerful that it became the foundation for an entire city. It is the story of the love Muhammad Quli Qutb Shah, the fifth Qutb Shahi ruler, had for a dancer named Bhagmati.

The legend goes that Quli met and fell in love with Bhagmati at the age of fourteen. So enamoured was he that he remained with her for the rest of his life despite severe opposition, first from his father and later from his court and the keepers of his faith. Over time, Quli's father Ibrahim became perhaps the only person to understand that Quli's love for Bhagmati was deeper than mere infatuation. When Quli defied a fierce storm and rode across the raging Musi river, simply to check that Bhagmati was safe, Ibrahim acknowledged the depth of Quli's emotion and ordered the construction of a bridge across the river. This bridge, four hundred years later, came to be known as the Purana Pul. Later, after Ibrahim's death and Quli's ascension to the throne of Golconda, the young sultan, it is said, married Bhagmati, made her his queen and built what is present-day Hyderabad, naming the new city Bhagnagar in her honour.

Whether or not the legend of Muhammad Quli and Bhagmati is based on truth is usually irrelevant to most Hyderabadis. The only thing that matters is the story. The belief that their home was built on love. Which is why, when I first read that political parties were flexing their muscles over the city's name, I was more than disturbed—I was alarmed. One political faction wanted the city's name to be changed to the original Bhagnagar/ Bhagyanagar, based not only on the dancer queen's name but also on the presence of a Bhagyalakshmi temple in the Charminar premises, while the other faction denied Bhagmati's existence altogether. If this political agenda is seriously pursued it could lead to a breach of the peace that the communities of Hyderabad have tried so hard to maintain over centuries. Now the city seems to be on edge, anticipating the slightest trigger for violent communal protests.

During the years I lived in Hyderabad, I fell in love with the city and its people. In those years, I heard a lot about the Qutb Shahis and especially about Bhagmati, the Hindu queen of the dynasty's fifth ruler, Muhammad Quli Qutb Shah. Their love story survived four centuries, and the number of tales surrounding it provided me with enough fodder to contemplate writing a romantic novel. But a couple of years ago, when people began talking about changing the name of the city, all thoughts of romance fled from my head. Instead, I felt an almost visceral need to explore Hyderabad's foundation story to the best of my ability. *Everyone,* I thought, *every person*—politicians, scholars and, above all, the people of Hyderabad—urgently needed to remember that for centuries the city had carried a legacy of communal harmony and had built for itself an insulated universe of cultural brotherhood, constructed at least in part on foundations laid by the Quli-Bhagmati love story.

I am not Hyderabad born and bred. But this allowed me the liberty to explore the Muhammad Quli-Bhagmati love story without bias and to present it as it should be perceived—as the genesis of a multicultural, multilingual and multi-religious ethos. To anyone who has spent a reasonable amount of time in Hyderabad—and anyone who is thrilled by stories rooted in history—it is clear that the relationship formed between the Muslim sultan and the Hindu dancer some five hundred years ago symbolises a composite culture that, despite the city's various changes of fortune over the centuries, remains strong even today.

Academics and historians are not just quick to dismiss Bhagmati's role in the foundation story of Hyderabad, they deny her existence altogether, citing the absence of any historical evidence of her presence in Muhammad Quli's life. Yet all over Hyderabad, people talk about Bhagmati and the love she shared with the sultan. As I delved deeper into the subject, I concluded that there were gaps in the narrative that historians refused to even acknowledge, let alone investigate. These gaps, if not filled, will continue to cause conflict and debate.

Documented history is important, but so are the hand-me-down folk tales that bind the people of a region together and bring its history alive. Folk tales represent the collective memory and beliefs of the people and are narrated without the biases that documented sources often display. Historian Ian Austin says in his book *City of Legends: The Story of Hyderabad*, 'Legends are traditionally-told stories of earlier times. Usually, they are non-historical and unverifiable, but being popular, they are too often accepted as historical record.' It is a fact that every contemporary traveller or official, residing in and around Hyderabad in the days of Muhammad Quli and after, has mentioned Bhagmati in some document or the other, or has indicated that the new city was originally called Bhagnagar. So why have modern historians, over the years, denied her existence?

In seeking the answer, I followed the advice offered by scholar and musician Srinivas Reddy in his book *Raya: Krishnadevaraya of Vijayanagara*, about the need for any writer of history, whether academic history or popular history, to examine a wide variety of sources so that the clearest picture possible of the subject in question may emerge.

'... For millennia,' Reddy wrote in his magnificent book on the south Indian king, 'Indians have recorded their past in creative ways, through sculpture, inscription, myth, poetry and songs. These sources may be deemed soft in the hard discipline of history, but if read in the right light, they offer fascinating historical insights found nowhere else.'

Thus, while I spent two years sifting through oral history references, cultural representations, books and manuscripts, gazettes and periodicals, contemporary sources including biographies, documented reports of travellers as well as commissioned projects, and transcripts of my conversations with intellectuals, scholars, journalists, heritage enthusiasts and old Hyderabad families, I also visited museums and monuments, examined paintings and read poetry to gather all the information I could find about Bhagmati. No definitive evidence emerged from this great mass of material proving the existence of the dancer and the love she shared with Muhammad Quli. But it is significant that I found no categorical evidence proving the opposite either. So the truth of Hyderabad's foundation story remains inconclusive and the book I have written, which draws upon both popular beliefs and hard facts, reflects this.

Meanwhile, for most Hyderabadis, the story of Bhagmati and Sultan Muhammad Quli will always bear repetition if for no other reason than the fact that it represents, in many ways, the spirit of the city. To make it a political issue will not only violate the soul of Hyderabad, causing irreparable damage to the city's cultural heritage, it will also break the big Hyderabadi heart.

CHAPTER 1

450 Years Ago

For fourteen-year-old Muhammad Quli Qutb Shah, the day started as it usually did with a ride within the environs of the Golconda Fort. Heading south, he galloped across the rocky terrain of Telangana, pleased with his life. The favourite son of Ibrahim Shah, the Sultan of Golconda, Quli was blessed with striking good looks—the very 'image of beauty', according to Sheikh Sharif Ahmad Gujrati, who has described the young man in his masnawi[1], Yusuf Zuleikha, *in this way:*

> The fresh growth of beard on his face
> Was like Raihan (a fragrant plant) from heaven
> No one has seen a shadow fall
> On the face of the sun
> His eyebrows arch like scimitars (katari), eyes dark and lively just like a maiden's
> His nose is straight like an alif and teeth like gems
> His fingers are adorned with rings, his mouth full of betel juice, fingernails coloured with henna
> His slender waist is very appealing
> Curly hair, tall like an alif, small mouth.[2]

Quli enjoyed his ride in the countryside, away from the fort that swarmed with traders, technicians and artisans from all over the region as well as Turkistan, Arabia and Persia. By now, the town within the fort's approximately eight thousand metres-long protective wall was so congested that his father was considering building a new city south of the river. But this was not an issue that the young man had to deal with. At fourteen, he had arrived at that stage in life when life itself was thrilling. Beautiful girls were everywhere and the whole of creation, it seemed, danced in delight, drunk on the sweet, heady nectar of love. He often spilled his emotions on paper, and in fact, was turning out to be quite a master of words as his poems show:

The beauties roam everywhere
dressed in their finery and adorned with jewels
They count the stars at night or play in the gardens
Some sing, some laugh, some dance,
some drink wine and some serve to others,
some are vividly intoxicated and happy.[3]

In this state of mind, when Quli chanced upon Bhagmati, a young devadasi making her way to the Nagamalleswara temple, his heart did not stand a chance. Love at first sight became a love that lasted all eternity.

Bhagmati lived in the village of Chinchlam across the Musi river from Golconda and often danced at the Nagamalleswara temple. Quli would return to meet her again and again and again. In the first flush of love, the young prince could not contain his emotions. He wrote:

The God of love, the clouds, the forests
are all masth (intoxicated with joy);
the wind, the breeze, the weather are all masth[4].

Though much older than Quli, Bhagmati started returning his affections and before long, the two became inseparable. News of the romance reached the sultan's ears. Normally, Ibrahim was an indulgent father, but Quli's romance with Bhagmati appeared to him to be something too serious for an adolescent. Worried, Ibrahim confined his son to his quarters in Balahissar in the fortress of Golconda and provided him with a bevy of beauties to seduce him away from his infatuation with the rustic commoner. These beautiful women came from all over India, as well as Arabia, Persia, Armenia and Turkey—lured by Ibrahim's announcement that whoever won the prince's heart would marry Quli and become the queen of Golconda. But Quli's heart remained with Bhagmati.

One night, after a week of heavy rain that left the Musi river in spate, the young prince, worried about his beloved Bhagmati, climbed onto the terrace of the palace, trying to look for lights in Chinchlam village, but the whole area was dark. Not one lamp flickered in the storm. Could the village have been washed away? Was Quli's Bhagmati lost to him forever?

Desperate to find her, the prince escaped his confines and ran to the stables where he mounted an elephant and then, dashed towards the swollen river. As guards rushed after him, Quli urged the beast into the foaming waters, but it refused to move. Desperate, he jumped off the elephant, pushed a soldier off his horse and, leaping onto the horse's back, plunged into the furious river, fighting the current to cross it. By the time Ibrahim heard of Quli's escapade and rushed out of the fort to stop him, the young prince had already crossed the Musi and was well on his way to Bhagmati's village.

Defeated, Ibrahim resigned himself to Quli's adoration of the dancer and decided that since he couldn't prevent his son from undertaking dangerous stunts to meet his lover, it would be wiser to facilitate his meetings with her than to lose him altogether. So he decided at once to build a bridge over the Musi river. The construction of this bridge cost the treasury Rs 1,00,000. As centuries passed, it came to be known as the Purana Pul.

India has its fair share of royal love stories. While the romance of the Mughal emperor Shah Jahan and his wife Mumtaz Mahal and that of the Maratha Peshwa Baji Rao I and his Muslim concubine Mastani was happy and fulfilled, other similar romances ended in gut-wrenching tragedy. The courtesan Anarkali, for example, beloved of the Mughal prince Salim, was buried alive by her lover's father, Jalaluddin Mohammad Akbar, the emperor of Hindustan.

But Muhammad Quli, who lived around the same time as Salim, though thousands of miles away in the Deccan, was luckier in love. His father not only facilitated his son's meetings with his lover, but even died early, clearing the way for Quli to bring his village belle home and make her his wife.

With a penchant for extravagance, Muhammad Quli built an entire city for his beloved Bhagmati, a woman whose religion, profession and social status were far removed from his royal lineage. This city he called Bhagnagar. Then, ignoring all opposition, he made Bhagmati his queen and conferred upon her the title Haider Mahal. From this title came the name of the city, Hyderabad.

As much as the origin story of their city makes Hyderabadis smile, Bhagmati suffered much the same fate as Anarkali. While she may not have been buried alive by her lover's powerful father, her name does not figure in any record of the Qutb Shah dynasty despite her status in legend as Muhammad Quli's wife and queen—perhaps his only wife and queen. Every trace of her

Bhagmati (Photo courtesy: Nathan Hughes Hamilton on Flickr via Creative Commons from his album 'Samples of India')

existence has been wiped off the official historical record, leaving her to become a part of folklore rather than a figure of history. Today, like Anarkali, Bhagmati occupies what the French historian Alain Désoulières calls a 'quasi-mythical' space.[5]

Note the word 'quasi'. Though no historical evidence has been found even for Bhagmati's existence leave alone her place in the heart of the fifth Qutb Shahi sultan, few historians, whether professional or amateur, dismiss her completely. While official records make no mention of her, the legend of Bhagmati's relationship with Quli runs so deep in the soul of Hyderabad that the search for her historical existence will likely continue for as long as the city survives.

However, if Bhagmati did exist and if she truly owned Quli's heart, it begs a question: why would a man who loved a woman so dearly as to defy all protocol to marry her and make her his queen, allow her name to be erased from public memory? Several contemporary chroniclers noted that Muhammad Quli enhanced Bhagmati's status to one worthy of a queen by providing her with an escort of a thousand cavalry—'certainly an unprecedented act of love in the annals of Golconda ... From this extraordinary expression of love leading to the elevation of her status, it looks as if it were directed against the rigid antediluvians and the foul-mouthed scalawags in order to overawe them into silence and submission that would obliquely contribute to boost up her morale, befitting his royal dignity.'[6]

As the sultan of Golconda, Quli could have overridden all attempts to hide Bhagmati from the public eye. So what kind of a man was he that he allowed his beloved to be erased from the historical record? Just as important, what kind of ruler was he? To understand Quli's predicament, we must trace the path he followed from the days of adolescent indulgences to his role as the fifth sultan of the powerful Qutb Shahi dynasty of Telangana.

The river of youth is now in flood
Mohammad Qutb Shah is now a young man.

In his masnawi *Qutb Mushtari*—a metaphorical romance he composed in 1609—Asadullah Wajhi, the court poet during the reign of Sultan Abdullah Qutb Shah, the seventh Qutb Shahi sultan, gives an elaborate description of Muhammad Quli as a prince in the prime of his life. Told in the dastaan[7] style, this romantic tale revolves around the sultan and his mistress Mushtari, the latter of whom we will discuss in a later chapter.

Vedagiri Rambabu's book *The Story of a Great City* (translated from Telugu by Sai Prasad Alahari) tells us that when Muhammad Quli was born, he was proclaimed a harbinger of good fortune for the kingdom of Golconda. That did not mean he was entitled to the throne—Ibrahim Qutb Shah had thirty children in all, with six sons and three daughters alive at the time of his death. So to succeed his father, Muhammad Quli needed the support of court nobles, who in turn would muster public support for his cause.

Raya Rao, a confidant and advisor of the late sultan, was one of Quli's biggest supporters. This was possibly because Rao was a leader of the Deccan group—a group of native nobles—who might have wanted Quli as the new sultan since he had a Hindu mother.

It is said that Raya Rao was so strongly in favour of seeing Quli on the throne that he even produced a purported will in which Ibrahim nominated Muhammad Quli as his successor. This seems unlikely since Muhammad Quli was not Ibrahim's eldest son, but whether or not there was a genuine will, Raya Rao produced one and used it to 'manipulate the enthronement' according to historian Narendra Luther.[8]

Muhammad Quli had two older brothers. The eldest died before Ibrahim's death, leaving the second-eldest, Hussain Quli as the next in line to the throne. Hussain Quli was the favoured candidate of Golconda's prime minister, Mir Shah Mir, since Hussain was betrothed to his daughter. But whether by providence or design, Mir Shah Mir was locked in a battle against Bijapur at Naldurg at the time of the coronation and, in what historian and author H.K. Sherwani insists was a coup,[9] the throne of Golconda went to Muhammad Quli. Hussain Quli lost not only the throne but his bride to his brother. Unable to bear the humiliation, he drowned himself in a tank.

Muhammad Quli was now the undisputed sultan of Golconda—and the husband of Mir Shah Mir's daughter. But he was still just a boy.

Born in 1565, according to Luther, Muhammad Quli would have been just about fifteen years old when he became Golconda's sultan (Rambabu says he was fourteen years and seven months old when he ascended the throne). According to the contemporary Persian historian Muhammad Qasim Hindu

Shah Astarabadi, better known as Ferishta (sometimes spelt Firishta), Muhammad Quli ascended the throne when he was even younger: 'This prince, on the death of his father, ascended the throne of Golconda in his twelfth year,' Ferishta has written. This is fervently disputed by Sherwani, who says, 'Muhammad Quli was born on Friday, 14-9-973/4-4-1566; Ferishta is wrong when he says that the prince was 12 when he ascended the throne, and also the fact that he was the eldest son of his father. Ferishta has committed many mistakes in his description of Qutb Shahi history, and Muhammad Quli in particular.'

He may have been twelve or fifteen, but nevertheless he was far too young to be entrusted with the duties of a king, so Muhammad Quli was led by his prime minister and father-in-law, Mir Shah Mir, who thrust him into his first battle in 1580-81, almost immediately after his ascension. This was against Adil Shah of Bijapur at Naldurg, which, at that time, had already been under siege for a year.[10]

Both contemporary and modern historians confirm that the battle at Naldurg was a 'venture that was not successful'. Luther says that after a year at Naldurg, Muhammad Quli broke camp, left his army in the field under his general Mustafa Khan and returned to Golconda. Three months later, according to Ferishta, 'Mustafa Khan ... was totally defeated by an army sent from Bijapur under the command of Dillawer Khan ...'

However, Sherwani believes that 'the campaign against the Adil Shahi forces at Naldurg [was] successful' and notes that celebrations followed this success. 'The celebrations in Golkonda *(sic)* included many a dance and song party and the atmosphere of the capital became heavy with the smell of exotic perfumes from all parts of the Orient,' Sherwani has written.

Sherwani also believes that Muhammad Quli married Mir Shah Mir's daughter *after* this 'victory', which led to more celebrations in the kingdom. But contemporary accounts and later historians say that Muhammad Quli, who married Mir's daughter at the time he ascended the throne, was so angered by his prime minister's poor judgement in taking Golconda to war, that he dismissed Mir summarily and sent him packing, along with his daughter, to Persia.

While Sherwani makes no mention of Mir Shah Mir's departure, historians such as Luther and Sha Rocco, who quote Ferishta, believe that having had a taste of war and governance, Muhammad Quli, though still a teenager, subsequently proved he had what it took to be a sultan. He invaded and took over Penugonda and Gandikota, extended the boundaries of his kingdom to Srikakulam, repaired any previous damage inflicted on his warring neighbours and, following his retreat from the Naldurg campaign, swiftly mended matters between Golconda and Bijapur. In 1586, after thwarting an impending offensive from Dillawer Khan, the regent of Ibrahim Adil Shah II of Bijapur, Muhammad Quli made good his commitment of marrying his sister Chand Sultana (not to be mistaken with the other Chand Bibi, the regent of Ahmadnagar) to the Bijapur sultan, thus establishing peace with his immediate neighbour.

Wars and politics apart, the commerce of Golconda flourished. Diamonds, steel and printed cloth attracted merchants from Asia and Europe. Fabric of various qualities and grades was produced in abundance and exported abroad. The art of Qalamkari or Kalamkari—a type of hand painted cotton textile using natural dyes—flourished in Masulipatnam and Narsapur. (In fact, kalamkari artwork is popular in the region even today.) Other kinds of textiles were also manufactured in and around Golconda.

Rajamundry's muslin was believed to be as fine as that made in Dhaka and Warangal. Ellore manufactured carpets that were in great demand in Persia and other foreign countries. Golconda was well known for the quality of its iron and steel too. Arms and armaments such as guns, spears, daggers, swords and blades were manufactured locally as well as domestic tools like knives, sickles, ploughs and spades. The kingdom's long coastal border also made for a well-developed ship building industry, which was much admired by international traders. According to employees of the East India Company, the ships made in Golconda were so strong that they could sail from the Coromandel coast to faraway places like Achin, Priaman, Queda, Perak, Ceylon and the Maldives. All this made the Qutb Shahi kingdom economically strong.

By 1586, six years after his father's death, Muhammad Quli was well ensconced in his throne, barring a few niggling threats. Bhagmati often visited him at his palace, accompanied by the cavalry of a thousand horsemen that he had assigned to her.

Ay Qutb Shah
Nabi ke sadqe mein Bhagmati se mil kar ...
Khud ko Qutb Shah ki dasi samajh kar khoob sajsaja kar ayi hai.

Oh Qutb Shah!
By the grace of Nabi, you have met Bhagmati ...
She who has dressed up just for you.[11]

Four years later, when he was fully settled on the throne of his kingdom, the sultan was ready to make Bhagmati his wife.

Wedding Procession of Sultan Muhammad Quli Qutb Shah circa 1650 (Photo courtesy: *Golconda/Bagnagar/Hyderabad: Rise and Fall of a Global Metropolis in Medieval India* by Serish Nanisetti)

Muhammad Quli Qutb Shah had loved his luxuries as a boy and continued to love them as a man. To enjoy the pleasures of life therefore, he made it a policy to avoid any sort of conflict, whether with other kingdoms or within his court. This was a weakness, he acknowledged, but he wasn't embarrassed by it and, in fact, wrote:

Wine and the company of woman is all I want
I have vowed to do only this in my life.[12]

For Quli, life was one continuous celebration. Every festival found a place in his poetry, not for its religious or spiritual aspects, but because it was a social event that brought him face to face with beauty. 'Shab-e-baraat (or Shabraat) is more like a bridal night,' he wrote, referring to the night when Muslims ask

Allah to forgive their sins. He made much of his own birthday celebrations too, writing ten poems about them. He had a way with words and was a compulsive writer of verses. In his thirty-year-long reign, he composed about fifty thousand couplets, which works out to about two thousand couplets a month or one hundred and fifty couplets a day. This filled him with such pride that he even wrote a couplet about that:

By the Grace of the Prophet, Qutb Shah composes verses every day
Just like waves rippling in a river.[13]

Quli's poetry was always about the happier emotions. Not for him the grim aspects of love—longing, yearning and despair. His verses were lavishly embellished with the physical and sensual, and depicted union, joy and merry making. He never experienced the sorrows of separation or any kind of despair, and the city he built reflected the same spirit and energy:

The city is verily a paradise
There is nothing that is not to be found
If an old man hurries to the city
He would recover his youth
Everything that is good is found in
Hyderabad in plenty
We find in the city all
That is fortunate and nothing that
Causes pain and sorrow.[14]

Beautiful women, of course, figured greatly in his life and in his verses, Quli often compared them to birbahutis or red beetles.

... They walk with swaying gait
Even the clouds and the breeze join them.[15]

But he also wrote specifically about his beloved—an unnamed woman who was possibly Bhagmati.

I cannot live without seeing my beloved
My body feels relaxed when we meet
Pleasant breeze, how do I pass the time without her?
Bring her to me so that I'm fulfilled.[16]

This unnamed woman so captivated the Sultan of Golconda that he repeatedly mentioned her in his verses more than any other woman. He described her beauty in great detail and acknowledged her special place in his life.

Dancer, your image is in the pupil of my heart
You are always sought after by my eyes
Waking and sleeping I can see only you
Wherever I look I see you standing.[17]

In his poems, Quli often addressed the unknown woman as 'dancer'. This is believed to be a reference to Bhagmati because she was a dancer—a devadasi or servant of God. She lived in Chinchlam, a predominantly Brahmin settlement where the Sufi saint Shah Chirag also had his abode. In Chinchlam, the cult of Mathangis followed the tradition of offering young girls as devadasis to temples, writes Rekha Pande in her paper *Writing the History of Women in the Margins: The Courtesans in India*. In the Hindu kingdom of Vijayanagar, which had been Golconda's neighbour before it was wiped off the map in the battle of

Talicota in 1565, the devadasis were of great importance as they served the gods. They were well versed in dance and music and were patronised by both the state and the public. The English merchant and administrator William Methwold, who visited Golconda during the reign of Muhammad Qutb Shah, recounted in his memoirs *Relations of the Kingdome of Golchonda and other Neighbouring Nations,* that during the festival of Ram Navami, 'They [the devadasis] would dance before the chariots of the Gods that would be taken out in a procession around the towns and villages.'

Not to be mistaken for courtesans—the women who entertained high-ranking men of the kingdom—devadasis were well mannered, enchanting and well read. In the book *Medieval Andhra: A Socio-Historical Perspective,* author Alpana Pandey, quoting historian Sarojini Regani, notes that Chowdappa, a Brahmin karnam (records keeper) from Cuddapah, had written that dancing girls were employed in all functions of society. No religious or social function was complete without devadasis. This was corroborated by contemporary European travellers, one of whom was quoted in W.H. Moreland's *Relations of Golconda in the Early Seventeenth Century* as saying, '... they [the devadasis] have to come regularly twice a day to dance in the temples in return for which they receive some annual gratification.'

Though devadasis enjoyed special privileges and honour, Pandey explains in her book that most of these girls acted as prostitutes to the Brahmin priests of the temple. In the Kaikkolam caste, for example, a girl from each family was dedicated to the village deity and she had to offer herself to the temple servants. According to Pandey, all the Brahmin priests had Kaikkolam girls attached to them. Members of the royalty and the nobility also often adopted these women as slaves and courtesans. As per Edgar Thurston and K. Rangachari in their book *Castes and Tribes of Southern India,* 'such women who were beautiful did enjoy a high status and were sometimes even gifted to royal personalities or monarchs.' Many devadasis were wealthy enough to donate large sums of cash to charity, Thurston and Rangachari add. They include in their book an amusing anecdote about a Sanskrit poet who, in the Travancore Census Report of 1901, described dasis of the Coromandel coast as 'walking flesh trees bearing golden fruits'.

With the arrival of Muslim rulers however, devadasis lost their special position because fewer temples were built and many were demolished. Even where temples remained intact, Muslim rulers did not patronise them, nor were they interested in patronising devadasis. Though the locals tried to continue the tradition, temples found it difficult to bear the expenditure of maintaining devadasis, and many of the women were forced to take to prostitution in order to survive. With the arrival of European travellers, who made no distinction between devadasis and regular dancing girls, the position of devadasis in the kingdom of Golconda further deteriorated, even though they could read, write and sing as well as dance.

The Devadasi system was exploited to the maximum during the medieval ages under an aggressive feudal hierarchy. The caste of Bhogamwar in the tracts around the Coromandel coast specialised in music, song and dance. Historian K.S.R. Murti, in his article *References to Bhagnagar in the Contemporary Telugu Literature of Qutb Shahi Period, and the Enigma of Bhagmati and Bhagirathi,* says that Bhagmati most likely belonged to this stigmatised caste. But the simple incident of birth into this caste didn't necessarily make Bhagmati a prostitute. Even so, Mughal chroniclers, who were prejudiced against all Deccan kingdoms due to an imperialistic snobbery, maligned Bhagmati by calling her a fahisha or a patare, which in simple terms meant whore or prostitute.[18]

There are different opinions about Bhagmati's caste though it may be said that with some accuracy that she belonged to a lower caste. At least two historians believed that Bhagmati belonged to the Arundhatiya community, which categorised itself as shudras and offered girls to the local temples as devadasis. Rekha Pande quotes columnist and writer Sri Pasam Jagannadham Naidu who has asserted that Bhagmati was 'an Arundhatiya damsel'. Historian and Hindi-Urdu writer Anand Raj Varma, the author of the book *Dastaan-e-Hyderabad*, also insists in a conversation with me that Bhagmati belonged to the Arundhatiya community based on his memories of the time when performers from Bhagmati's erstwhile village of Chinchlam visited his ancestral home, as they did the houses of all local jagirdars and other wealthy people, to sing bhajans during the festivals of Diwali and Dussehra. Since Chinchlam, where Muhammad Quli first encountered Bhagmati, was a place where the cult of Mathangi, as per the religious custom of shudras, dedicated girls to temples as devadasis, it is almost certain that Bhagmati was from this community.

According to folklore, Bhagmati would perform at the Nagamalleswara temple, about two hundred kilometres from Golconda, and Muhammad Quli saw her for the first time one day while she had been on her way to the temple. Other stories claim that Quli saw her at a temple dedicated to Bhagyalakshmi (the Goddess of Fortune) somewhere near Chinchlam. Often, writes historian Sita Anantha Raman in the first volume of her book *Women In India: A Social and Cultural History*, the names of devadasis reflected the names of the temples or towns to which they were attached, so it was highly likely that a dancer called Bhagmati had danced at a temple of Bhagyalakshmi.

The truth, however, is that there is no real evidence even of Bhagmati's existence, let alone her profession. Journalist and social activist Mir Ayoob Ali Khan, whose family has lived in Hyderabad for several generations, insists in a conversation with me that even though people from the Chinchlam region regard Bhagmati as a devadasi even today, she was actually a nautch girl. He reasons that by the time Muhammad Quli came to power, the devadasi tradition was already in decline, given the fact that Muslim rulers had been ruling in the Deccan for several generations by then.

According to historian K.S.R. Murti, it is the anti-Bhagmati lobby which is guilty of 'dubbing Bhagmati as a street woman or demi-mondaine ... a woman of doubtful reputation and standing, belonging to the outskirts of society ...' For instance, Muhammad Hashim (1664-1732), an Indo-Persian historian of Mughal India who was better known as Khafi Khan, has said very clearly in his *Muntakhab-al Lubab* that Bhagmati was the wife of Muhammad Quli ul Mulk, who at her request built for her a new city called Bhagnagar. But the Persian text version of *Muntakhab-al Lubab* says, 'Sometime after Bhagmati's death, objection was raised to the name of Bhagnagar on account of its disgraceful origin and the city was given the name of Haidarabad. But in the vernacular language, it is still called Bhagnagar.'

Whether she was a devadasi or a nautch girl, legend has it that Bhagmati was intellectually gifted and talented, famed for her skill in playing musical instruments, singing and dancing and for being both literate and fluent in Telugu, Dakhni and Persian.

Romance of Kings and Commoners in Golconda by Dr Rahimuddin Kemal—a translation in English of Dr Mohiuddin Qadri Zore's Urdu works *Golconde ke Heerey* and *Sair-e-Golcunda*—makes this point. If true, this made Bhagmati Muhammad Quli's intellectual equal, but her faith and her position in society worked against her. Though the twenty-four-year-old sultan was deeply in love with Bhagmati, he knew that if he wanted a peaceful kingdom that left him with enough time to enjoy his women and write his verses, he needed to keep all factions of his court happy, including friends, foes and above all, nobles and the Muslim clergy. He was under no illusion that a Hindu wife would be accepted as queen by his immediate coterie of ministers, especially a woman who, unlike his own mother, a princess of Vijayanagar, was a commoner and of a lower caste. (However, while some reports say Quli's mother was from a Brahmin family, others insist she was from a community of entertainers and that Ibrahim had married her only after her conversion to Islam.)

Aside from this, Quli was a staunch Shia, who constantly reinforced his commitment to his faith. Immediately after his accession to the throne in 1581, according to historian Sayyada Jafar, he added the symbol of the Alam (flag) on his coins, which reflected 'his deep faith in Imam Hussain'. Many of the verses he wrote focussed on his devotion too. Seven of his poems, for example, are manqibats[19] of Hazrat Ali and more than a dozen poems are on topics such as Id-e-Maulud-e-Ali and Id-e-Ghadir.

Qutb Shah is the slave of the twelve Imams.
He is your devoted slave, Ali, help him.[20]

In his verses, Quli often expressed loyalty towards the Shias. According to his successor and son-in-law Sultan Qutb Shah, who was also the first person to compile Muhammad Quli's diwan,[21] 'He never concluded a ghazal without remembering Hazrat Ali.'[22]

Though he was known to be quite liberal in matters of faith and never forced his subjects to convert, Quli's verses reflected his growing sectarian biases at times. He was, after all, surrounded by staunch Shias like Mir Momin Astrabadi, Golconda's new prime minister, and Mirza Muhammad Amin Shahristani 'Ruh al-Amin', a leading Iranian poet who was appointed as the Mir Jumla. The latter was at the helm of both civil and military affairs until the sultan's death.[23]

More likely though, this was a part of his dynastic longing to please the Shah of Iran. Like his grandfather Sultan Quli, Muhammad Quli eagerly welcomed immigrants from Persia and introduced the name of Shah Ismail Safavi in the Khutbah.[24] The Persian immigrants helped establish extensive commercial and trade relations between Golconda and Persia. 'The greatest respect and profits are obtained by the Persians, a nation exceedingly haughty and self-regarding, beyond all other Indian nations,' said an anonymous employee of one of the European trading companies.[25]

Masulipatnam, on Golconda's eastern border, was a major port at the time and a throbbing hub of trade between Golconda and Persia right through the one hundred and seventy years of the Qutb Shahi rule. Textiles, gunpowder, tobacco, rubies and wooden furniture went to Persia and silver, carpets, glass, pearls, fruits, horses as well as material for books and book binding returned to Golconda. Slaves were both exported and imported.

It wasn't just Persian goods that flooded the state. Professionals like civil engineers, architects and skilled artisans also immigrated to Golconda, while physicians trained in the

Greco-Arab school of Unani medicine arrived to set up practice. (A Unani hospital exists close to the Charminar even today.) Teachers and tutors for royal students were Persians who used the Persian system of education that was considered the best possible model, since the elite and top positions in the Golconda administration were occupied by Persians.

In many ways, Golconda was virtually an intellectual colony of Persia, so it wasn't surprising that some years later, when he decided to build a new city, Muhammad Quli was urged by Mir Momin Astrabadi to base the design on the Persian city of Isfahan.

Records show that Anthony Schorer, an employee of the Dutch factory in Masulipatnam who visited Golconda between 1609 and 1614, wrote to the directors of his company that, 'The king of Golconda bestows large sums in religious benevolence, especially on Persians, who come from Persia in great numbers, men of noble ancestry but small means.'[26] The Persian domination of all matters in Muhammad Quli's kingdom was also noted by the Englishman Floris whose account was printed in Samuel Purchas's *Purchas His Pilgrimage Or Relations of the World and the Religions Observed in All Ages and Places Discovered from the Creation Unto This Present*. Floris, after recording the death of Muhammad Quli in 1611 and the succession of his nephew Muhammad Qutb Shah to the throne, wrote of the latter, '... his uncle (Muhammad Quli) had put all in the hands of the Persians ...'

It was no wonder, therefore, that Muhammad Quli became obsessed with the expression of Shia ideology, such that he abused Sunnis, inviting in the process the opposition of Sunni nobles and the Ulema. He graphically described devastating scenes from the battle of Karbala in his elegies, set up a langarkhana in the sacred memory of the Imam and even prayed for the downfall of the Sunnis.

The idol houses of the kafir Sunnis have fallen at this hour
Now they are afraid of the unforeseen
We are Shias and all the Sunnis are our enemies
Ali, son of Abu Talib, fell them with a blow of your hand.[27]

Many of Quli's couplets brutally attack Sunnis and reflect his zealotry:

I have pierced their hearts with arrows
The Sunnis are jealous of me
I have conquered both the worlds
I have no one but you, O Ali.[28]

Occasionally, Muhammad Quli's pen targeted Hindus too, even though he had a Hindu mother and a Hindu lover, celebrated Hindu festivals and wrote verses on Hindu women. Some portraits also show him dressed in the Hindu style, in an angvastram and a pagri (turban) with an embroidered sarpech. Yet, he has written:

The faith of the prophet survives
You chase out the Hindu armies
Destroy the darkness of sin
Bring forth the sparkling daylight.[29]

Given this extreme devotion to his faith, it is not difficult to imagine Quli being torn by conflicting emotions when it came to Bhagmati. But passion won over faith at least for some time and he made Bhagmati his queen, despite the consternation of his nobles and his prime minister.

I feel heady with love, in the company of my beloved
My feet, my walk and my movement are all ecstatic
By the Grace of the Prophet, Qutb is enjoying his days and night
the breeze, the wine, his entire countenance is ecstatic.[30]

Love, romance, beauty, pleasure and abundance were recurring themes in Muhammad Quli's verses. His compositions reflect his obsession with the physical and are limited to his own experiences of lovemaking. He was a 'slave of pleasure' says Masud Husain in his book *Mohammad Quli Qutb Shah*. A worshipper of beauty in all its forms, he drew inspiration from the bevy of women who surrounded him all the time. Books and philosophy—he had no time for those.

What have I learnt from books?
I have after all learnt the language
of rosy cheeks and dark tresses.[31]

'Quli was not a scholar of books but of beauty, of physical beauty,' says linguist and Dakhni Urdu scholar Masud Husain. Quoting Ali Bin Tabatabai, who served Ibrahim Quli Qutb Shah and chronicled his experiences in a book called *Burhan-e-Maer*, Husain says that among the sons of Ibrahim, Muhammad Quli was exceptional. 'His individualism lay in the domain of poetry. He was not interested in questions of philosophy or Islamic theology (tasawwuf) and his poetry lacks in philosophical thought.'

Quli was not ashamed of this. He wrote of his own education (or the lack of it) in the following verse:

I am an ummi (uneducated person), but my words are my pen though I cannot write.[32]

In a show of humility, Quli even called himself unlettered, though it is unlikely that a sultan with an oeuvre like Quli's could actually be illiterate. The following lines give an example of Quli's confidence in his own literally skill:

By the Grace of the Prophet, Qutb has composed poetry in all bahrs (metres)
Other poets have not equalled him.[33]

There are several misconceptions in the minds of contemporary historians regarding the upbringing and education of Muhammad Quli, probably because compared to his two elder brothers, his education was rather unconventional.[34] Perhaps because Quli's mother was a Hindu and his father had spent many years in the Hindu kingdom of Vijayanagar, his parents had not been particularly interested in Quli's Islamic studies. Left to himself, the young prince had pursued pleasure. He had followed his heart and the advice of his immediate coterie of religious and political ministers instead of pursuing the more strict and arduous discipline of scholarship. But what he lacked in formal education was more than compensated for by his talent in poetry.

For Quli, poetry was a release, at once intimate and revealing. His critics were not as enthused. Professor Masud Husain has said about Quli, 'He does not know what sublimity is and is blissfully unaware of the need for thought in sensual love.' Some of his poems could even border on the graphic.

Your two breasts are like the palaces of heaven
Your lips like a pitcher of wine.[35]

According to Masud Husain, Muhammad Quli 'was not so proficient in his description of human nature as he is of the emotions and desires which are aroused in his heart ... and his inner feelings and other forms of enjoyment are the experience of physical pleasure'. Perhaps he was able to write without restraint because he was the sultan, thus often 'crossing acceptable limits'. And perhaps this frankness, this possible obscenity, prevented him from gaining his due fame as a poet.

While the names of other poets from the Deccan find mention in the memoirs or works of contemporary poets, Quli's name figures nowhere. Even the poets of his own court, such as Wajhi, Gawwasi and Sheikh Ahmad Gujrati, don't mention him while talking of poets of the time, nor do they applaud his poetic skills in any manner. They have praised him for his patronage and appreciation of poetry, but not one word has been said about his poetry. Ibn-e-Nishati, the seventeenth century Dakhni poet in the court of Sultan Abdullah Qutb Shah, has named four masters from the Golconda School of poetry in his book *Phool Ban*, but Quli does not figure on the list. This could not have been a lapse—after all, Quli had been the sultan and the patron of the four masters! But Quli never compelled his fellow poets, even those in his service, to acknowledge his poetic abilities, nor did he expect any kind of flattery or sycophancy from them. Rather, he graciously acknowledged the influence of other poets on his work—Dakhni poets such as Mahmud and Firuz and Persian poets such as Hafiz, Anwari, Nizami, Khaqani, Unsuri and Zahir Faryabi. In one of his qasidas (odes), *Qasida-e-basant*, he openly mentioned Khaqani's influence:

God has gifted you the delicate art of composing poetry
Maani, is this your sher or one of Khaqani's?

(Maani was one of the several takhullus or pen names that Muhammad Quli used in his verses.)

Even later poets did not believe that Muhammad Quli's poetry was particularly special. The noted Urdu poet and scholar Firaq Gorkhpuri observed about Quli: 'Sensuality and love if they are pure and simple can lead to the creation of relatively better love poetry, but truly great love poetry is not possible from a man whose interest is confined to sheer sensuality and love.'[36]

Whether or not his fellow poets acknowledged the worth of his verses, Muhammad Quli did not care. Perhaps he was the ideal writer, writing not for fame or posterity, but because he enjoyed writing. In one verse he wrote:

No one can write commentary on my works
I'm unique among all.

Only three hundred years later was his poetic talent recognised when Maulvi Abdul Haq, a man whose passion for Urdu earned him the sobriquet Baba-e-Urdu or Grand Old Man of Urdu, rediscovered Quli's poetry. Haq presented Quli's diwan in his journal *Risala-e Urdu*, and called Quli the first Urdu poet, thus dethroning the reigning title holder Wali Mohammad Wali, known until then as the Father of Rekhta and the Chaucer of Urdu poetry.[37]

'Muhammad Quli was the first to write in the style of Persians and to collect a diwan in alphabetical order after their manner—an honour hitherto assigned to Wali,' says Ram Babu Saksena in his book *History of Urdu Literature*. According to Haq, Quli's efforts led to the birth of the Persian poetic style and its usage in the Dabistaan-e-Golconda—Golconda's literary school of thought. Muhammad Quli, it turns out, nurtured Dakhni Urdu from its infancy to create a unique poetic tradition that reflected two distinct styles of Urdu poetry—the Persianised style of the Golconda School and the Hindawi style of the Gujarat and Bijapur Schools.[38] So much for his lack of education!

Haq's contemporary, the poet-scholar and literary critic Mohiuddin Qadri Zore, has raised Muhammad Quli even higher, hailing him as the father of Urdu poetry. Jalaluddin Mohammad Akbar, Ibrahim Adil Shah and Muhammad Quli Qutb Shah, Zore has said, were the 'standard bearers of the unique Ganga-Jumni culture'. To this, Luther adds, 'That led to excessive adulation for him [Quli] and the tone adopted by some writers and commentators of that period, notably Dr Zore, was so full of praise giving an impression that they were his court chroniclers.'

Even so, Muhammad Quli's poetry puzzles psychologists and literary critics alike. 'Can pleasure seeking and a strong religious bent of mind go together? We find this kind of strange union between lust and religious fervour in the poetry of Muhammad Quli ... In one breath, Quli writes of sex and then prays to the Prophet or Hazrat Ali for help ... Even at the moment of ultimate ecstasy which he calls "apar aiyas", Quli did not forget to thank the Prophet,' says Masud Husain. Was this merely a mechanical observation by Quli or was this religious fanaticism?

Perhaps the pre-Victorian era in which Muhammad Quli lived

found nothing wrong in talking about sex and God in the same breath. Perhaps Quli was simply a very passionate man. Only the latter can possibly explain the giant leap he took when he married Bhagmati in 1589, almost a decade after he first met her.

Over the next ten years, two major events unfolded in the lives of the sultan and his queen Bhagmati. First, the birth of their daughter Hayat Bakshi Begum who came to be known as Ma Sahiba and wielded influence over the next three generations of Qutb Shahi sultans. Second, a plan that would change the map of not just Golconda, but all of Telengana and even alter the history of the Deccan. That meant the building of a new city, one that would not only accommodate the growing population of Golconda, but act as a homage to Quli's beloved Bhagmati; a thriving, throbbing symbol of life representing the bond of eternal love.

The city Quli created four hundred years ago stands just as strongly for multiculturism and ethnic pluralism today as it did at the start. It also stands for a love that will never die. As Maqdoom Mohiuddin said in his poem *Bhagmati:*

Shahr baaqī hai mohabbat kā nishāñ baaqī hai
Dilbarī baaqī hai dil-dāri-e-jāñ baaqī hai
sar-e-fahrist nigārān-e-jahāñ baaqī hai
tū nahīñ hai terī chashm-e-nigarāñ baaqī hai.

The city remains a mark of your love,
Friendship and love remain.
At the top of the list is your name
You are not there. You may be gone, but your watchful eyes remain its sentry.[39]

CHAPTER 2

The Reluctant Kings

Long before the birth of Hyderabad, before Golconda was even a word let alone a fort, before the Qutb Shahi dynasty came into being and the tale of Muhammad Quli Qutb Shah and his dancer queen Bhagmati entered the hearts of the inhabitants of the region, romance imbued the atmosphere of the Deccan.

Perhaps the reason for this glamour was the nature of the region. The Deccan is home to some of the oldest rocks on planet Earth and it is replete with gold, diamonds, and other gems. A place such as this naturally attracted attention and, especially after value started being assigned to stones and metals, the Deccan became a region of mystique and alluring stories, inviting adventurers and travellers from all over the world to visit.

Medieval adventurers such as Marco Polo, who visited India in the thirteenth century, and his fellow countryman Niccolo de Conti, who travelled to India two hundred years after him, established a strange but plausible connection between the stories of the Arabian Nights and the fort of Golconda.

In his book *A Guide to Golconda Fort and Tombs*, Hargrave Jennings, a nineteenth century British author who wrote on occultism and esotericism under the pseudonym Sha Rocco, has quoted Marco Polo's description of this district when the Italian traveller had visited Queen Rudrama Devi of Warangal in 1292.'He [Marco Polo] mentions Sindbad's story of the eagles and joints of mutton,' writes Jennings. 'Writing of Golconda, he [Marco Polo] said, "the flower of the diamonds and other large gems; as well as the largest pearls, are all carried to the great Koos and other kings and princes of those regions. In truth they possess all the treasures of the world".'

In the same book, Sha Rocco has quoted Niccolo de Conti who visited Vijayanagar in 1420 or 1421: 'Diamonds were found on a mountain which he [Conti] called Albenigaras and brought in the story of Sindbad. Apparently, the mines to which he referred were those on the banks of the Kistna river. They were known as the mines of Golconda.'

Whether or not the glittering valley Sindbad referred to in his story was really Golconda, we cannot know. But it is certainly true that the sparkle of the kingdom lured adventurers and conquerors alike. 'Jewels of great emperors flash in its very consonants,' wrote Sha Rocco.

In fact, English poet John Keats opened his poem *On Receiving a Curious Shell, and a Copy of Verses, from the Same Ladies* with the following lines:

Hast thou from the caves of Golconda, a gem
Pure as the ice-drop that froze on the mountain?
Bright as the humming-bird's green diadem,
When it flutters in sun-beams that shine through a fountain?

If you walk amidst the sprawling ruins of Golconda today, you might hear the stony sentinels whisper tales from five hundred years ago of a kingdom that epitomised all that was opulent, luxurious and romantic. 'It might have come out of the Arabian Nights; its kings could have led a life in which Harim-al-Raschid would have found himself at ease,' says Sha Rocco in his book.

Not just Golconda, but the whole of the Deccan seemed to be on the list of most adventurers, whether private or those working as emissaries of kings at a time when each kingdom in the region was wrestling with another. By the end of the fifteenth century, the Hindu kingdom of Vijayanagar was flexing its muscles to combat the ever-growing threat of Muslim dominance, while its Muslim neighbour, the house of the mighty Bahmanis, was tottering. From the ashes of the Bahmani empire, five new kingdoms arose, including that of the Qutb Shahis of Golconda whose kings were considered as powerful as those of their once mighty neighbour Vijayanagar.[1]

By the time of the first battle of Panipat in 1526 when the Mughals arrived in North India, the first sultan of Golconda had already laid the foundation of a formidable dynasty and fortified the mud walls of a three hundred-year-old or even older fort, a Kakatiya relic, turning it into a structure that would become one of the most important landmarks of Deccan history.

According to Sha Rocco, there is no recorded history of Golconda before the year 1364. But traces of the citadel indicate that the Golconda fort is at least as old as the fort of Warangal, which dates from the middle of the thirteenth century. Probably Golconda was originally a small mud and brick fort belonging to a local chieftain before it fell under the sway of the Warangal rajahs. The fort we are familiar with now was first built by the Kakatiya rajahs of Warangal, particularly Ganapathi Deva in the thirteenth century, but in 1464, when the Kakatiya rule ended, the fort was ceded to the Bahmani ruler Muhammad Shah III Lashkari. More than a hundred years later, in 1501, Sultan Quli, the first Qutb Shahi king, was appointed the governor of Telangana by Shihab-ud-din Mahmud Shah Bahmani II, who reigned between 1482 and 1518, and the fort fell within his domain.

In 1518, Sultan Quli began reconstructing it in granite and renamed the area around it Mahmodnagar. Some sixty-two years later, in the reign of the fourth Qutb Shahi king, Ibrahim Qutb Shah, the reconstruction was finally completed. Because of Ibrahim Qutb Shah's addition of stone and lime to the materials of the reconstruction, the Golconda fort has survived both the ravages of time and the plunder of man. The fort sits poised atop a four hundred feet-high hill, and has a circumference of approximately eight kilometres including eighty-seven semi-circular bastions, each fifty to sixty feet high. Eight huge gates—Fateh gate, Makka gate, Patencheroo gate, Banjara gate, Jamal gate, Moti gate, Bahmani gate and the New Fort gate—allow entry and exit. The Fateh gate led to military and defensive structures, a mortuary, baths, silos, mosques, gardens, residential quarters, pavilions, royal courts, royal palaces, mosques, bazaars, arsenals and the Madanna temple built for Hindu courtiers. Within the important Balahissar area of the fort were the Silahkhana, Nagina bagh, Ambar khana, Ramdas jail, Darbar hall, baradari and hamams. There were cultivated fields and water tanks within the confines of the fort. In times of danger, a major part of the population, both Hindus and Muslims, would take refuge inside the fort, hoping that the fifty-feet wide trench around its outer wall would keep them safe.

Though it never took centre stage in the political history of the region, the Qutb Shah-led kingdom of Golconda, which was created from the fragments of the Bahmani empire, has left a legacy that has survived five centuries. The fort in the Qutb Shah domain grew to become an opulent, dazzling kingdom

Golconda Fort (Photo courtesy: Moupia Basu)

that was 'destined to play a much more important and lasting part in Indian history,' according to J.D.B. Gribble in his book *A History of the Deccan*. Amidst the constantly fluctuating fortunes of the Deccan's mini kingdoms that were forever realigning their frontiers, Golconda's destiny seemed to follow a more fortuitous trail as much by providence as by design. In terms of location, it was unobtrusive, tucked away in the eastern corner of the sprawling Bahmani kingdom. But it served as the headquarters of the Telangana province and was a lucrative destination. 'There was booty to be gained,' says Gribble.

Golconda's diamonds were famous all over the world. But its bustling ports of Masulipatnam and Cocinada on the Coromandel coastline were just as attractive to adventurers. This strategic location, in fact, may have contributed more to Golconda's expanding fortunes than any diamond mine.

Perhaps this was because Golconda did not actually have a diamond mine. Not within its territory, not even within a hundred kilometres of the fort! The much vaunted diamond mines, in fact, lay scattered across the surrounding districts of Kurnul, Cuddapah and Nellore and the diamonds were brought to the royal fort of Golconda from those places. But merchants and traders from across the world presumed that the stones were found in Golconda itself, which led to various stories and legends that prompted kings and commoners from across the world to seek their fortunes within the fort.[2] Laden with such wealth, or tales of wealth, it was no wonder that the kingdom of Golconda, partly by default and partly by strategy, pushed its rank and that of its governor higher than that of its neighbours in the Deccan.

Sultan Quli Qutb Shah or Sultan Quli, the patriarch and founder of the Qutb Shahi dynasty who ruled between 1512 and 1543, became the governor of Telangana just as the Bahmani empire began to flounder. Bestowed with the title of Sultan Quli Qutb-ul-Mulk by his lord and benefactor the Bahmani sultan Mahmud Shah, Sultan Quli never took advantage of the political situation to declare his independence and proclaim his kingship, unlike the other governors of Bahmani-held regions. This is attested by the inscription on his grave that simply says, 'Sultan-Quli, Qutb-ul-Mulk'. The word 'sultan' was never a title. It was only a part of the name given to him at birth.

Considering his several accomplishments, it was quite unusual for a young man of his stature to *not* seek an independent royal title. Was it a lack of ambition or simply loyalty to his king? Probably neither, given the circumstances under which he had come to India with no clue of what might await him in this alien land. Sultan Quli's arrival in his adopted country arose more from a quirk of fate than any purposeful agenda. He had been a refugee of sorts, devoid of ambition or intention.

Quli had fled his homeland of Saadabad in Humadan to escape the clutches of Hasan Beg, the amir of Aq Quvinlu (the white sheep), the arch enemy of his own tribe of Qara Quvinlu (the black sheep). On Quli's birth, it was prophesied that he would one day become an emperor. When he learned of this, Hasan Beg's successor Amir Yakub hatched a plot to kill the boy. Urged by well-wishers, Sultan Quli's father packed him off to India, accompanied by his uncle Allah Quli. Little did the young Sultan Quli know that this seemingly unfortunate turn of events would mark the beginning of a completely unforeseen and unplanned journey that would push him and his descendants into the pages of Hindustan's history, that they would forever be remembered for altering the map of southern India and spearheading an intellectual movement that would embellish India's cultural fabric for centuries to come.

Hindustan welcomed the boy and his uncle and they eventually landed up in the court of the Bahmani king Shams-ud-din Muhammad Shah III Lashkari who ruled between 1463 and 1482. Sultan Quli had a favourable initial stint in the Bahmani kingdom. When some petty landowners and inhabitants refused to pay revenue, Quli volunteered to resolve the issue without troops. He was successful in his mission and managed to recover many small districts that had been reclaimed by the Hindus. When his uncle left Hindustan to return to his homeland, Shihabu'd-din Mahmud Shah, the son of Muhammad Shah III Lashkari, who had become the new Bahmani king after his father's demise, insisted that Sultan Quli be left behind, promising to treat him as his own child. Sultan Quli's skills in mathematics had already been recognised and Mahmud Shah tempted him with an appointment as the royal accountant, thus preventing his early departure from India. Quli, who was already in awe of the splendour of the Bahmani kingdom, was more than happy to remain where he was. Impressed with his military and intellectual talent, Mahmud Shah awarded Sultan Quli a liberal annuity and subsequently recruited him in the body of his favourite courtiers. When a hunting incident went in favour of Sultan Quli, Mahmud Shah granted him one hundred and fifty Arab, Turkish and Iraqi horses, assigned him the jagir of Kurangal for his expenses and also bestowed upon him the title of Khawas Khan. Quli in his turn served his lord with a fierce loyalty, suppressing all kinds of uprisings including dacoity and non-payment of taxes.

As the years passed, Sultan Quli became so famous for his accomplishments that a firman (edict) was issued proclaiming him a master of the sword and the pen. Successful military campaigns between 1474 and 1496 earned him the title of Qutb-ul-Mulk and later that of Amir-ul-Umara. Several subsequent military victories saw him rising in prestige and power. In 1487, he quelled a rebellion in Bidar arising from the Bahmani sultan's appointment of several Turkish and Iranians in important positions. The local population of Deccanis were outraged and revolted against the sultan, seizing the Bidar fort and attempting to assassinate him. When Quli saved Mahmud Shah's life, he was rewarded with grateful loyalty from his master. In 1494, Mahmud Shah sent Sultan Quli on a campaign to punish Goa's thanedar, Bahadur Gelani. Quli defeated Gelani in the Battle of Panhala and earned the title of Qutb-ul-Mulk. In 1495-96, Quli took over as the subedar of Telangana and with that he acquired the jagirs of Warangal, Kodangal, Golconda[3] and the strategic Golconda fort.

Over a period of time, Sultan Quli earned as much love and respect from the people of Telangana as he had from Mahmud Shah. He made Telangana his home and strengthened the existing fort of Golconda—the fort lies eight kilometres from the centre of the current city of Hyderabad—naming the area around the fort Mahmodnagar after Mahmud Shah Bahmani and making it his headquarters.

The conflict between the Persians and the Deccanis eventually led to the fall of the Bahmanis. While the subedars of Ahmednagar and Bijapur immediately proclaimed their independence, Sultan Quli desisted and instead helped his sultan wage a war against Bijapur by sending forces to his aid. Whether it was diplomacy, prudence or loyalty, Sultan Quli never once considered himself an independent ruler, at least not officially. This helped build a strong foundation for the dynasty. Barring a few instances, the Qutb Shahi rule was one of the most peaceful reigns in Indian history until the arrival of the Mughal emperor Aurangzeb. It was only after Mahmud Shah's death in 1518 that Sultan Quli declared his independence and shifted his capital to the Golconda fort. While still acting as a Bahmani representative, he had keenly studied the problems faced by Mahmud Shah and was careful not to make the same mistakes that the Bahmani sultans had made. A peaceful reign got him happy subjects and the local population grew fond of their new ruler.

Sultan Quli ruled for fifty years, as a governor for the first twenty-four years and later as a ruler for twenty-six years. At the time of his assassination, the kingdom of Golconda stretched from Warangal to Masulipatnam. Though he was himself a Shia, Sultan Quli waited until the accession of the Shia Shah Ismail Safavi to the throne of Iran in 1501 to introduce Shia Islam in Golconda. He gradually replaced the names of the three caliphs with the names of the twelve Imams. Shah Ismail's name was introduced in the Khutbah and Shia-ism was thus established as a state religion.

Even in the most illustrious lineages, the path to glory is invariably smeared with blood. Often the blood spilled is that of a kin. While Sultan Quli cannot be said to be guilty of harming any close relative, the career of his son and successor Yar Jamshed was drenched in familial gore.

Yar Jamshed, who ruled between 1543 and 1550, was ruthless with his relatives. First, he blinded his older brother Khutbuddin and, in all probability, would have killed him had he not been caught. Thereafter, he killed his own father while the latter knelt in prayer. Having started with blood lust, Yar Jamshed's reign was one of discontent and conflict, greatly exacerbated by enemies who urged his brothers to fight for the throne. When Jamshed's brother Ibrahim Qutb Shah, who had been appointed as Golconda's heir by their father, attempted to take the throne with the help of the Bidar sultan Ali Barad, Jamshed was quick to retaliate. Though he did first try for a peaceful resolution by offering Ibrahim the post of the chief commander of his army, but when Ibrahim turned down the offer, Jamshed got the Sultan of Ahmednagar to attack Bijapur, making Ali Barad flee, which left Ibrahim with no choice but to make a dash for Vijayanagar. Jamshed then bribed Sardar Narayana Pandit, an independent chieftain, to prevent Ibrahim from reaching Vijayanagar, but the Vijayanagar king, Aliya Rama Raya, forced Narayana Pandit to release Ibrahim, who he then took with him to Vijayanagar and provided with a jagir.

Yet, when Burhan Nizam Shah of Ahmednagar sent his envoy to congratulate Jamshed on his accession and offered him a crown and the royal umbrella of kingship, Jamshed turned down the honour, saying that he had never aspired to royalty and would not be a sultan as long as he lived. Like his father, Jamshed never declared his independence from the Bahmani empire. His grave boasts no epitaph nor can any coins issued by him be found anywhere, barring a doubtful few with the name Janshibd.[4] The Qutb Shahis started minting coins very early but did so only very rarely, and those minted seem to have been simply curiosities, not currency. Many scholars are wary of authenticating the coins or of attributing them to Jamshed Qutb Shah and his son Subhan Quli Qutb Shah.[5]

It is strange that a man with a lust for power did not want to be recognised as a king. In Jamshed's own words, which he is believed to have composed spontaneously for Burhan-ul-Mulk, he wished to simply remain a governor.

'I do not need a royal canopy, nor do I crave an honorific title at this old age. Because the kings of the Deccan, one and all, have held the canopy of kingship in their name only then when by their valour and magnanimity and by the strength of their arms and (power of their) intellect, they carried the ball (of victory) from the (control of the) treacherous sky, out of the plain of valour with the help of the mall-stick of battle. Then alone will I accept a title and a crown when I will reveal to the king the striking strength of my valiant hand. Then alone will I accept the regal insignia (chatra) when through the grace of the Prophet I seize it from the enemy,'[6] Jamshed is known to have said.

Kingship aside, Yar Jamshed was determined to rule Telangana. Unfortunately for his subjects, Jamshed had a cruel disposition and a decadent lifestyle. The only saving grace was that his reign lasted just seven years, though the last two years were apparently nothing short of terrifying. A man of violent passions, Jamshed 'sank into gross debauchery'.[7] However, he was a fairly decent poet—a poet by 'inclination', according to the scholar T.N. Devare—and some of his works may be seen in the Tazkira of Kalamul Muluk (by Saadat Ali Rizvi) and the historical account of Hadaiq-us-Salatin.[8]

The reign of Jamshed's son and successor Subhan Quli Qutb Shah lasted all of six months. Just seven years old when he ascended the throne in 1550, the boy shortly passed into such obscurity that he does not even seem to have a grave.

Meanwhile, Jamshed's death brought Ibrahim Qutb Shah, the fourth son of Sultan Quli, back to Golconda. But his return to his father's stronghold was a reluctant one. By all accounts, Ibrahim had been happy serving the king of Vijayanagar. He had spent a considerable part of his time in the company of Telugu poets and littérateurs, while at the same time learning the art of administration from his close proximity with Aliya Rama Raya. So, he was in no mood to leave Vijayanagar for Golconda. For a while, Ibrahim found reprieve when the Naikwaris—Hindu aristocrats such as Jagadeva Rao, the naikwari of Kaulas, and Jagapat Rao—backed his younger brother Daulat Khan as a contender for the throne. But Daulat Khan insisted that only Ibrahim deserved the honour of kingship. Pressed by the nobles and Naikwaris of Telangana, Ibrahim relented and entered the city of Golconda on 27 July 1550, welcomed by a jubilant throng of well-wishers including the Karkuns, officers, Naikwaris, blacksmiths, oddas, well-diggers, guards, load bearers, bandsmen, tenants and other Hindus and Muslims who hailed him as Malik Ibrahim Shah, the new 'king'. He was the first of the Qutb dynasty to be so proclaimed.[9]

Ibrahim's coronation was grand. He sat on a golden throne flanked on both sides by a golden chair. Gold statutes of a lion and an elephant were placed on either side, to symbolise the might and majesty of the state. The new king adopted sky blue as the official colour of the kingdom and a tricolour ensign was created by incorporating red, sky blue and white. With Ibrahim's coronation, the Qutb Shahi kingdom entered its most glorious period, one that would continue for the next sixty years, first under Ibrahim himself and then under his son Muhammad Quli. The bloody skirmishes, murders and incidents of treachery that had marked Yar Jamshed's rule were over.

The Qutb Shahi rulers were not aggressive conquerors. Yet, each time the need arose, they crushed those who rose in rebellion and displayed superb political foresight. Ibrahim, who ruled for thirty years, consolidated his kingdom while extending its boundaries. He strengthened the Golconda fort with stone and mortar and added a double rampart with a circumference of eight kilometres. The renovation and strengthening of the fort cost him Rs 2.1 million. A man of hedonistic tastes, he built some impressive structures, dotted the capital with tanks and laid out several flower gardens. But not once did he allow his love for aesthetics to interfere with his governance.

The first in his dynasty to be called a king by his contemporaries and 'the first to whom some undisputed coins can be traced', according to Sherwani, Ibrahim was an able administrator and a sharp diplomat.[10] His political acumen and military skills prompted him to eventually join the league of the Deccan sultanates and defeat his one-time benefactor, Rama Raya, the king of Vijayanagar.

By 1564, Rama Raya's influence had spread far and wide and, taking advantage of his supremacy, he became an arbitrator of the quarrels between the Deccan sultans. Unfortunately, as time passed, his disposition changed and he apparently became haughty and overbearing, and started ill-treating the sultans.[11] This was too much for Ibrahim Qutb Shah, who invited all the sultans to form a league against the Vijayanagar kingdom. While the sultans of Bijapur, Bidar, Ahmednagar and Golconda joined hands, the sultan of Berar stayed away. The armies of the Deccan sultans and that of Vijayanagar met at Rakkas Tagadi near Talikota on 25 January 1565. The Vijayanagar army, comprising one hundred thousand horses and three hundred thousand infantry fought, bravely. But once Rama Raya was killed and his head was paraded on a spear, his army, having suffered the loss of a hundred thousand men, fled in confusion. The Muslim armies pursued them and entered Vijayanagar where they stayed for six months and destroyed the once glorious and mighty kingdom.

The repercussions of the battle reverberated through the length and breadth of the Deccan, altering the fortunes and the borders of the Deccan sultanates. The spoils were unfairly divided, with Golconda and Bijapur bagging the larger shares of the booty. The kings of both Bijapur and Golconda annexed erstwhile Vijayanagar districts on their southern borders and advanced their boundaries to the area that later became Madras. Meanwhile, Golconda not only pacified the rebellion-ridden north-eastern frontier of the kingdom which extended up to what is the present-day Andhra-Orissa border, but also secured for itself Masulipatnam, the prized trading hub on the east coast.

Right from the beginning of the collapse of the Bahmani empire, Golconda witnessed less action than its more ambitious neighbours. Sultan Quli seemed to have a lack of interest in conspiracies, plots and political drama, and this was a trait that continued right down his lineage. None of the Golconda sultans was interested in the affairs of other kingdoms, and they always kept to themselves unless called upon to engage in the disputes of their neighbours, especially those of the constantly warring kingdoms of Bijapur and Ahmednagar.[12]

Whether this strategy was deliberate or a result of Qutb Shah sultans actually preferring peace to aggression, it paid rich dividends. The very fact that Sultan Quli was the governor of the much prized and coveted 'booty' of Telangana was due to his loyalty to his master: he had been given Telangana as a token of appreciation. But peace and pleasure seemed to have meant more to the Golconda sultans than politics and power. While perfectly capable of ensuring that their own interests were well protected, each one of them used literature, language and art as tools to generate aesthetic and artistic wealth and to establish, not just communal harmony, but also a multilingual, multicultural and multi-religious tapestry that binds together the inhabitants of the region even today.

This did not mean that the local Hindus and Muslims did not clash at all. In the infancy of the Golconda kingdom at least, there were incidents of discontent between the followers of the two faiths. For example, the *Tarikh-i-Muhammad Qutb Shahi* mentions that all the Hindu temples in the Devara Konda region were demolished on the orders of Sultan Quli, once the fort there had been captured, and mosques were built on the ruins. Thus, it appears that the Qutb Shahis' reputation as benevolent and tolerant rulers was restricted strictly to their own subjects and territory; different rules seemed to apply in cases of war and invasion. According to an inscription dating back to 1584, Ibrahim Quli occupied the Ahobilam temple assisted by some Hindus. The same inscription indicates that for about six years, while the region was under the Qutb Shahi rule, no worship took place in any of the temples in the region while, according to the Kaifiyats (village registers) of Sudipudi and Veleru, temple construction halted in the region during the time the Qutb Shahis occupied the southern coast. There were also instances of idols being buried by Hindus to protect them from attacks.[13]

There are other reports of communal conflict as well. For instance, when Ibrahim Qutb Shah suddenly died, a rumour did the rounds that blamed the idols of Hindu gods for his death. The story, according to Sha Rocco, is that Murari Rao, a Maratha Brahman entrusted with the management of state affairs, marched with some troops towards a famous temple near Adoni and after killing all the inhabitants, robbed the temple of its gold and silver idols and gems. The idols were brought before Ibrahim Qutb and as soon as he lay eyes on them, he took seriously ill and died soon after. Hindus believed this to be the vengeance of their gods, while Mohammedans referred to it as the demonic power of idols.

Contrary to these reports however, W.H. Moreland has remarked in his *Relations of Golconda in the Early Seventeenth Century* that the inhabitants of the region were almost entirely Hindu and spoke Telugu. 'I find no record of conversion to Islam having taken place on a large scale in this region, and the bulk of the resident Moslems must be regarded as of foreign origin, whether merchants who had settled at the seaports or soldiers and adventurers who had followed the flag from the North,' Moreland wrote.

Though pushed into kingship, Ibrahim quickly assumed dominance over the Tilang-Andhra region and sorted out the chaos created by his predecessor Yar Jamshed. His reign was a long and eventful one, during which the kingdom of Golconda came into its own politically. At the same time, Ibrahim Qutb Shah's court witnessed a burst of literary activity, 'brought about by the patronage given to Telugu as well as Persian, and the slow but sure rise of the Dakhni idiom which later flowed into Urdu.'[14]

Ibrahim had Telugu luminaries in his court such as Addanki Gangadhara Kavi who was appointed the kingdom's poet laureate and who dedicated his work *Tapati Samvaranopakhyanm* to the sultan. Other poets included Kandukuri Rudra Kavi and Ponnikanti Teleganarya Kavi. *Sugriva Vijayam*, considered the first Yaksha Ganam in Telugu, was written during Ibrahim's reign. The Sultan also patronised other forms of fine art such as theatre performances of Yaksha Ganam in temples and elsewhere.

According to Addanki, Ibrahim's court was thronged by men accomplished in the Vedas, Puranas and the cognate sciences. He was probably the first Muslim ruler to whom a Telugu book was dedicated. In a bid to encourage poets and promote literary activity, Ibrahim presented poets with jagirs. For example, Kandukuri Rudra Kavi, the author of *Nirankusopakhyanam*, received the village Rentachinthala in Chintalepallam as a jagir. In patronising littérateurs, Ibrahim was only doing as his father had done before him. Among his many accomplishments, Sultan Quli had patronised the arts and initiated a tradition of grants to poets and littérateurs. One such recipient was Ellanna who was granted the village of Karkonda.

During Ibrahim's reign, several Telugu works such as *Chitra Bharatham* by Sarigonda Dharmanna and *Niroshtya Ramayanam* by Maringanti Singaracharyulu were also published. Ibrahim had ambassadors from the courts of Narapati of Vijayanagar and Gajapati of Orissa and many nayakas and chieftains from South India visited his court, according to Vedagiri Rambabu in his *The Story of a Great City (Nalugu Satabdala Nagaram)*.

Poets are known to usually praise kings and emperors during their lifetime, but Ibrahim Quli was praised in verse even after his death. This speaks volumes for the reputation he built as a connoisseur of literature. It is believed that Ibrahim was so captivated by the Deccani cultural identity that after he married the Vijayanagar princess Bhagirathi, he desired Golconda to be known as Bhagirathi Nagaram. No wonder his son Muhammad Quli decided to name the new city he built after his own wife, Bhagmati. Ibrahim also patronised Persian, Telugu and the Deccani idiom that later evolved into Urdu. (The Deccani or proto-Urdu language was the language of communication amongst people from different walks of life.) He was so enamoured of Telugu, the court language of Vijayanagar, that he 'vied with the Telugu-speaking rulers in his patronage of that language.'[15] He filled his court with Telugu poets and some of the highest posts in his kingdom were occupied by the Telugus. This endeared him to his Telugu-speaking populace to such an extent that he was affectionately called Malkibrama and Abhiram.

During his eventful reign of thirty years, Ibrahim managed to sire thirty children, of whom six sons reached maturity. By the time of his death, his first two sons were no longer alive (one had died by poisoning, the other by drowning). Ibrahim's third son ascended the throne of Golconda in 1580 and went on to rule for the next thirty years. This was Abu Muzaffar Muhammad Quli Qutb Shah (1580-1612), servant of the Prophet, the fifth Sultan of Golconda and the hero of this book.

Born right after the Battle of Talikota in 1565, Muhammad Quli's arrival in the world led to a gigantic celebration.[16] A chronogram was prepared for the prince and he was bestowed with the title of Bais-e-Rozi-e-Ahil-e-Alam: Provider of Sustenance to the People. The rejoicing was so great that the court poet Asadullah Wajhi described the events years later in his epic ballad *Qutb Mushtari*:

> Because in this gathering, angels had come to render service, the king gave them so much gold that they made a new sky of gold. The sky itself was given so much gold that it keeps on going round day and night to find a place to keep it. The earth itself was given so much wealth that it is begging heavens for space to keep it. After giving all these charities, the king himself celebrated the festival of spring with diamonds. On Muhammad Quli's birth, gold was distributed so liberally that it had become cheaper than dirt. So many jewels and gems were scattered all over that swans have started coming on land to pick up their food.

Ibrahim Qutb Shah believed that his son Mohammad Quli's moment of birth was propitious and that he was the harbinger of good fortune for the dynasty. This idea was not misplaced. Mohammad Quli Qutb Shah earned himself a reputation for having liberal leanings as well as the title of Saheb-e-Saif-o-Qalam: Man with Sword and Pen. Like his father, Muhammad Quli was proficient in Telugu and patronised Telugu poets such as Domakonda Malla Reddy, who was his poet laureate and the author of *Shat Chakravarti Charitra* and *Siva Dharmotharamu*.[17] Raja Mallareddy, a scholar of Telugu and Sanskrit, the poet Gananatha and Saarangu Tammaiah who co-authored *Vyjayanti Vilasamu*, also frequented his court. So proud were they to be part of the sultan's court that they mentioned it in their compositions. Quli himself composed poetry in Telugu, using the pen name Turknam. He held weekly literary discussions in both Telugu and Urdu and used several Telugu words in his Urdu compositions. And since he was well versed in the Telugu language and literature of the land he ruled, it was not unnatural for him to have fallen in love with a Telugu girl (Bhagmati) in his childhood.[18]

Historian Laura Weinstein notes that Muhammad Quli's poetry was deeply rooted in the Deccani regional culture,[19] liberally sprinkled with 'metaphors inspired by Sanskrit poetry'. He wrote in Dakhni, a form of Hindustani written in the Arabic script, with a vocabulary that mixed the Persian, the Arabic and the Indic. This was a commonly used language in the Deccan in the sixteenth century, especially in the realm of literature and poetry. Over time, with the patronage it received in courts, especially the court of Golconda, it became more and more refined, making creative alterations to the style while remaining within the parameters of Persian and Arabic semantics. Both the language and the subject matter of Muhammad Quli's compositions suggest an author deeply embedded in Deccani regional culture. Muhammad Quli was one of the earliest major poets in Dakhni and his decision to compose in this language reveals a great deal about his interests, inclinations, self-reflections and ambitions.

Though Quli's poetry mostly focused on happier emotions, he occasionally assumed the form of a *virahini*—a female pining for her lover. Laura Weinstein in her paper *Variations on a Persian Theme: The Dīwān of Muhammad-Quli Qutb Shah and the Birth of the Illustrated Urdu Dīwān,* quotes historian and scholar Carla Petievich who says that the tradition of writing poetry from the point of view of a female longing for her lover (the virahin)—a perspective frequently assumed by Muhammad Quli—was the quintessential and distinctive Indic element in Dakhni literature, just as it was in other early forms of Urdu. Petievich locates the origin of this practice of writing in the feminine voice in the literary tradition of North Indian Krishna bhakti poetry.[20] 'The presence of this female asiq (feminine voice) is almost certainly inspired by the virahini of Indic poetry and the significance of this inspiration should be neither overlooked nor underestimated. It indicates a recognition on the part of Dakhani poets that the virahini—who is the lyric voice of both Bhakti poetry and secular Indic love literature—represents an expression fundamentally similar to that of the Perso-Arabic tradition's asiq who suffers the throes of firaq-e-yar (separation from the beloved).'

Below is an example of Muhammad Quli's use of the virahini:

Sweetheart don't jerk me around, I'm already your slave
I've embarked upon the five-fold path with ease
Day broke as I passed the time with you on love's bed

My eyes are drunk on just your memory
O you of consummate charm, see how enslaved is this poor girl!
It was clear you robbed her of her senses
On account of you this universe ceased to exist for her.
By the grace of the Prophet you are Qutb's sweetheart
Go ahead, adorn yourself of deceit and trickery![21]

In this poem, not only has Muhammad Quli worked within the Indic tradition by writing from the point of view of a woman intoxicated and enslaved by love, but he has also mentioned the fivefold path which Petievich suggests may refer to an Ayurvedic practice of self-purification.

More importantly, Muhammad Quli's adoption of the Indic literary tradition points to his deep identification with the people of the soil. Though Persian from his father's side, his taste and observance of Indic traditions could have come from his Hindu mother and his Hindu wife, Bhagmati.

Quli celebrated seasons as well as festivals in his poetry. His ghazal *Dakhin Ki Barsaat* or *Rain in the Deccan* describes the splendour of the rainy season, his favourite of all weathers:

The season of flowers has come
The garden boughs are heavy with the crown of flowers
Holding a cup of raindrops in their hand
The rain maidens adorn themselves
Their limbs shiver with cold
Their youth full of thunder
They look at their lover out of the corners of their eyes
There is thunder and more rain.
In the garden of love the peacocks reign
By the Grace of the Prophet

The rainy season is here
Qutb Shah enjoy yourself each day.[22]

In the Deccan tradition, the rainy season commences on Mirag or Eid-e-Soori, a day when the sky turns a beautiful orange. It is always a day of merry-making and for Muhammad Quli it was a day of pure bliss, ushering in the season of musk and saffron, of amber and sandalwood, of pure revelry. Quli always asked his musicians to play raag Malhar on this day.

The season of the deer has come
Doe-eyed maidens roam around in their finery
Sing now with your full-throated voice
Like the koel
Drink the wine of the papiha's song
The grass is green, so is the cup,
The youthful bodies are also green
Youth itself is green and in the greenery
rivulets are stringing their crystal pearls.[23]

Such was the magic of the monsoon that in Quli's fantastical depictions, the maidens surrounding him were fairies and with his senses all fired up, he imagined the sound of thunder mixing with the melody of shehnai.

The clouds are thundering
Come on maidens, adorn yourself
The rain is falling with a sweet drizzle
wet your blouses in the rain
the earth and the sky
Seem to be of one colour

today is the day for rejoicing
Come, sing the raag malhaar
fill your ruby lips
With the wine of love and
offer them to your new king Mohammad Shah.[24]

Quli's interest in Telugu and Deccani Urdu combined with his liberal leanings made Golconda a shining example of what was later called 'Deccani culture': a blend of Hindu and Muslim cultural traditions that ensured a relatively peaceful atmosphere in the kingdom, shorn of conflict or strife until the arrival of Aurangzeb. This was no easy feat and it set the tone for Hyderabad's unique way of life that exists even today.

In a paper titled *Indo-Muslim Culture in Hyderabad: Old City Neighbourhoods in the Nineteenth Century,* historian and anthropologist Karen Leonard calls Hyderabadi culture an Indo-Muslim culture, deliberately using the word 'Muslim' rather than 'Islamic' to emphasise a civilisational culture rather than a religious one. The court, the administration and the daily life of the urban citizens of Golconda were all Indo-Muslim. The people, especially those who lived in the neighbourhoods of the old walled city, 'participated in that dominant public culture, regardless of their religious affiliations and private religious observances,' she wrote.

Names such as Jahangir Pershad and Fateh Chand were common. Kayasths, who are members of a high Hindu writing or administrative caste and who originally belonged to northern and western India, were well absorbed in the Qutb Shahi social system and continued their allegiance to their Indo-Muslim culture even during the British rule.

Ibrahim Qutb Shah's thirty-year reign had already altered the fortunes of the Qutb Shahi dynasty. With Muhammad Quli carrying forward the legacy of his forefathers, the kingdom of Golconda witnessed one of its most politically peaceful periods as well as a period of cultural and social renaissance.

About half a century later, when the Frenchman Jean de Thevenot stepped on the soil of Telangana, he remarked: 'The most powerful of the Kings of Deccan, next to Viziapour, is the King of Golconda. His kingdom borders on the East side, upon the Sea of Bengala; to the North, upon the Mountains of the Countrey of Orixa; to the South, upon many Countries of Bisnagar, or ancient Narsingue, which belongs to the King of Viziapour; and to the West, upon the Empire of the Great Mogul, by the province of Balagate, where the Village of Calvar is, which is the last place of Mogolisian, on that side.'[25]

Though better known as a poet and a builder than a gallant king, Muhammad Quli was proficient in all the skills required of him as a ruler. He was an able administrator and a shrewd diplomat who had no qualms in appeasing all factions if that meant the borders of his kingdom were secure and he had enough time to indulge his passions. It is no small task for a king to have offered his subjects a three-decade long just and peaceful rule via a fine balancing act between being a king and an aesthete.

Perhaps it was these very skills that impelled Muhammad Quli to allow the name of his beloved queen, Bhagmati, to be erased from history. As a king, there were certain sectarian, diplomatic as well as moral obligations that he couldn't ignore. But what he couldn't remove was the belief of the people who insist that the magnificent city of Hyderabad was built for her.

CHAPTER 3

Bhagmati's Bhagyanagar or Ali's Hyderabad?

Hyderabad jise shahr-e-nigārāñ kahiye
rañg-e-rukhsār sahr-e-husn-e-bahārāñ kahiye
kisī shāir ke ḳhayāloñ kī hasīn duniyā hai
gul-ezāroñ kī ġhazāloñ kī hasīñ duniyā hai
us kī mittī meñ mohabbat ke kañval khilte haiñ
zarre-zarre meñ dhaḍakte hue dil milte haiñ
us ke sine meñ qutub-shāh kā kirdār bhī hai
vaza-dārī bhī hai iḳhlās bhī hai pyaar bhī hai
us kī bāñhoñ meñ basī bhāg-matī kī duniyā
jagmagātā hai jahāñ chāñd ravā-dārī kā[1]

I recently read a delightful book called *Romance of Kings and Commoners in Golcunda* by the scholar and historian Rahimuddin Kemal. This is an English translation of Dr Syed Mohiuddin Qadri Zore's Urdu works *Golcunde ke Heeray* and *Sair-e-Golcunda*. In his introduction, Dr Kemal says that the book is 'a study of the life and culture of Golcunda interwoven into stories'.

Romance of Kings and Commoners in Golcunda consists of twenty stories about Golconda collected by Zore over years of visits to the ruins of the town within the fort and his meetings with the descendants of families that had lived there for generations. Kemal calls these stories, all narrated in Dakhni Urdu, historic and semi-historic, layered with the romanticism of each passing generation of storytellers. For me, these hand-me-down tales are as important as real events. They are a route to understanding the development of Deccani culture in Golconda and Bhagmati's role, if any, in this development.

Unlike their contemporaries in the north, says Kemal, all the kingdoms in the Deccan '... actively initiated the process of cultural synthesis. The elite cultural aesthetics and values found expression in life and institutions at the level of the common people. The kingdom of Golconda brought together Indo-Turko-Iranian cultural elements thus creating a new, vital and composite culture known as the Deccani culture under the Deccan sultanates—the Bahmanis followed by the Qutb Shahis and the other kingdoms in the Deccan.'

To understand this kind of a social and cultural climate, it is important to study the life, customs and traditions of the people of the Deccan as well as the region's recorded history. The political map may have changed continually with one kingdom replacing another, but each new kingdom inherited the earlier kingdom's cultural lineage and built upon it in the development of its own traditions and institutions. Cultural continuity was the thread that bound the Deccani kingdoms and oral traditions formed an unbreakable strand of this thread. Political events change constantly, but people are the true inheritors of any civilisational legacy, so it is important to explore the ethos, the spirit and the beliefs of the people when investigating history.

Many residents of Hyderabad are excellent storytellers, ready at a moment's notice to pull out fascinating tales from their rich repertoire of myths and legends. Kemal argues that though Zore was not a historian but only a scholar of Deccani literature, his studies took him into the realms of history and culture and he has, thus, produced an authentic history of literature. The stories Zore collected represent Golconda's culture, history and way of life. And of all these tales, the one that has never ceased to engage and bind the citizens of Hyderabad is the love story of Muhammad Quli and Bhagmati.

That the Muhammad Quli-Bhagmati story remains beloved despite its precarious provenance is obvious even now. Even the government-run 'son et lumière' show at the Golconda fortress is centred upon this love story. In fact, most scholars are more dismissive of Zore's belief that Muhammad Quli was the father of Urdu poetry than they are of the Bhagmati story. They acknowledge Bhagmati's status as the sultan's queen but feel that Zore was perhaps too emotional about the sultan's literary accomplishments!

However, Zore's near hero-worship of the sultan made Muhammad Quli popular in the twentieth century. So much so that H.K. Sherwani notes in his book *Muhammad-Quli Qutb Shah: Founder of Haidarabad,* that in 1958, Dr Syed Mohiuddin Qadri Zore, to recapture the glory of the reign and age of the fifth Qutb Shahi sultan, instituted a Muhammad Quli Qutb Shah Day, an annual celebration on 4 April, the sultan's birthday. This meant that the love story of the sultan and Bhagmati was back in focus. Sadly, the annual celebrations were discontinued a few decades ago.

While Zore's books do not always provide historical accuracy, they nevertheless offer alternative narratives that align themselves with popular culture. The myths and legends of folk traditions and oral histories remain persistent in the memories of people through generations and as much as academics and historians might dismiss these tales, they can do nothing about their popularity and mass appeal. In fact, studies by folklorists have frequently 'found some measure of residual truth in narratives persistently recounted over centuries,' according to Narendra Luther.

India is rife with legends that have found their way into people's hearts. Narrated again and again, some of these stories have become synonymous with the identities of the regions in which they are set. In this process, what is recorded as history is almost indistinguishable from what has been handed down through oral renditions of legends. Well-known intellectual and scholar Sajjad Shahid remarks in his paper *Interface of History & Fiction in Urban Legends: Told & Untold Stories of Hyderabad* that he has found this to be particularly true in the case of the Qutb Shahi dynasty. 'It, therefore, becomes all the more important to explore oral traditions and legends handed down through generations as a valuable source of information and not dismiss them completely,' he says.

Of all the legends associated with the Qutb Shahis, the Muhammad Quli-Bhagmati love affair, of course, tops the list. Since there is no commissioned documentation of this story, it may well be just a fairy tale. There is no historical evidence of Bhagmati's existence and her political status, but she has lived for nearly five hundred years as the origin story of Hyderabad and this makes her a compelling person to investigate.

The old city of Hyderabad comes truly alive during the month of Ramzan, when shops, restaurants and kiosks remain open through the night to cater to a population fasting for forty days. Visiting the city one time during Ramzan, I revelled in the brightly lit shops and stalls proudly showing off all kinds of goods. The bazaars were crowded, the vendors sang out their sales pitches and the night air carried both a mild aroma of spices and the strains of a ghazal wafting from an invisible location. At an hour past midnight, just after I had licked up the last bits of haleem and biryani at Shadaab Restaurant, I decided to walk through the crowds thronging the all-night bazaar to catch a glimpse of the Charminar, whose silhouette loomed up majestically just a little ahead of us. A dear friend of mine who had accompanied me on this midnight jaunt with her two daughters and husband was a tad nervous and decided to cover her head for safety's sake, which perplexed me because Hyderabad is a perfectly safe city. She stopped at a stall to buy yards of zari for her daughter's forthcoming wedding, while I continued to walk towards the Charminar.

The area around the monument had been cordoned off for some reason, but the magical aura of a love story persisted. Was this the spot where, according to the story, Muhammad Quli first set eyes upon Bhagmati? Or was that romantic place somewhere beyond the monument? Glancing at the clock on the wall of the Charminar, I saw it was 1.40 a.m. I don't know how long I stood there, admiring this magnificent structure, but suddenly I realised that the noise from the night bazaar was fading away.

I had read Dr Kemal's book only a few days earlier. Two of the stories were about Bhagmati. While the first was written by Zore himself, Kemal has added another story about the queen, this one from Bhagmati's perspective. This particular story will not find a place in the historical records, but it throws up several questions.

Kemal very cleverly brings Bhagmati's existence into the realm of possibility by blaming Mir Momin Asterabadi, Muhammad

Quli's Persian prime minister, as the person responsible for erasing the dancer's name from history. Though Sherwani refutes this vehemently, Kemal lends his voice to Bhagmati, allowing her to speak her own truth.

Hayat was her name. My lovely girl, my daughter. They took her away from me. She was given to a wet nurse from Persia and was brought up by Khanum Agha who was married to my master's [Muhammad Quli] brother. It was all the doing of Mir Momin who never liked me, or should I say never acknowledged me as the queen. He was not happy with the idea of a queen who came from common stock, who was a dancer. It was he who convinced my master to take our daughter away from me. Can you be more full of sorrow than I am?

Have you ever seen my name anywhere? Any coins, any inscription, anything as proof that I lived? They even said Hayat was my master's child from his first begum, the daughter of the previous prime minister Mir Shah Mir, whom my master sent away.

As I looked up at the Charminar in the growing quiet of the night, Kemal's account of Bhagmati's thoughts came alive. Amidst the twinkling lights of the city, I almost expected an apparition to loom up on the first storey of the Charminar. But there was nothing there besides the long shadows cast over the verandah.

The stories about Bhagmati are so numerous and interesting that it is impossible to believe the claims that she'd never existed. Though she had been dearly beloved by her husband and had been the queen of the kingdom, she has no grave to her name, neither at the royal necropolis, nor in her village.

A fake grave does exist though, in Shahalibanda, an area now occupied by a pehlwan (wrestler). Some very frantic scrambling had led to its creation overnight several decades ago when the then chief minister of undivided Andhra Pradesh had decided he wanted to visit Bhagmati's grave. But there is no known actual grave for Bhagmati, say old residents of the city. It is not even known whether on her death she had been buried or cremated.

The absence of a grave or a memorial to Bhagmati gives those who do not believe in the story of the dancer queen more ammunition against those who are convinced she existed. After all, as a heritage enthusiast explained to me, if Bhagmati had indeed been the fifth sultan's queen, there would certainly have been a memorial dedicated to her.

But relics associated with the love story of Bhagmati and Muhammad Quli are scattered across the old city of Hyderabad, including the Purana Pul that Muhammad Quli's father Ibrahim Qutb Shah is believed to have built to enable his son to safely cross the tempestuous river whenever he went to meet his beloved.

The construction of the Purana Pul was completed two years before Ibrahim's death in 986 AH (1578 CE). The story goes that Ibrahim, shaken by his son's daredevilry, had ordered that the bridge be completed before winter commenced. It took eight months to construct the bridge, which was paved with large flat stones. The chronogram engraved on it read 'Guzargahema' which means 'the water flows under the bridge and we pass above it'.[2]

The bridge might perhaps have been completed a couple of months sooner if it hadn't been for a stone mason named Rangayya. Rangayya, the story goes, disappeared from the construction site immediately after the basic framework of the bridge had been made, just as the process of curing the stone began. For weeks, there was no more work. All the labourers did was pour water over the stonework day after day. The sultan was incensed. He had wanted this bridge completed urgently to keep his headstrong son safe. But there was no sign of Rangayya.

Exactly two months after he had vanished, Rangayya turned up again. Bravely, he went directly to Ibrahim and patiently bore the sultan's wrath. Once it seemed Ibrahim had finally cooled down, Rangayya explained his absence. The stonework of the bridge, he told the sultan, had needed to be cured with water for at least sixty days to ensure its durability. Had he remained on the site during those sixty days, the sultan might have ordered him to complete the bridge regardless of the time required to cure the stone. Knowing he could never refuse an order from the sultan, Rangayya had decided to disappear so the stone could be properly treated. Amused by this explanation, Ibrahim forgave Rangayya and the bridge was soon completed.[3]

The gate that leads to the Purana Pul is one of the thirteen gates that led in and out of the city of Golconda. Over the years, most of these gates were destroyed and now only two remain, the Purana Pul gate being one of the survivors. This gate, apparently, was where Shivaji signed a peace treaty with the then reigning sultan, Abu Hasan Tana Shah, in 1677. It is made of wood with iron plates and nails and has an iron horseshoe attached to it. As per legend, some men, who had arrived in Golconda from Karbala, had offered two such horseshoes to the sultan, claiming that they had belonged to Hazrat Husain's horse and were therefore sacred. The sultan had accepted the horseshoes with the utmost respect and had got one nailed to this gate and the other to the ashurkhana at Pathargatti.

The Purana Pul, when it was completed, was called Siraat-ul-Mustakheem (straight road). It is the oldest bridge in Golconda/

Hyderabad and figures among the oldest bridges in India, thanks to Rangayya.

Jean-Baptiste Tavernier, the French traveller, who visited Golconda during the reign of Abdullah Qutb Shah (grandson of Muhammad Quli), thought the Purana Pul no less beautiful than the Pont Neuf in Paris. He was equally impressed by the town, which he described as 'nearly the size of Orleans'.[4] According to Tavernier, Golconda was a rich country 'abounding in corn, rice, cattle, sheep, fowls and other commodities necessary to life'. He also described the many tanks in the kingdom that had bunds or dams built on one side to retain water for the irrigation of agricultural fields in the dry season and that these water bodies were always filled with fish. In his book *A Short History of Aurangzib, Vol. 1*, Sir Jadunath Sarkar has written, 'To its smiling cornfields, tanks teeming with fish, and flourishing handicrafts, must be added the diamond and gold mines which made the name of Golconda known even in far off Europe.'

The construction of the bridge was Sultan Ibrahim's first step towards moving out of the Golconda fortress which by then had become heavily congested. However, he died on 2 June 1580 (988 AH) before he could carry out his plan to construct a new city, leaving behind a kingdom 'as prosperous as Egypt and like the mart of the whole world'.[5]

Twelve years later, Ibrahim's third son, Muhammad Quli, put the plan for a new city into action. While out hunting one day, he crossed the bridge and came across an expanse of land that he quite liked. Unlike the hill upon which the Golconda fortress perched, this area was flat and green, bordering the river. The area was pleasing to the eye and moreover was much closer to Chinchlam, Bhagmati's village, than Golconda.

Excited at the prospect of moving closer to his beloved, Muhammad Quli at once set upon the task of drawing up the blueprint for a new city, an idea his father had nurtured for years. Ibrahim Shah had extended the capital in his lifetime, but towards the west of Golconda to a place that at the time was known as Muhammadpuram. The name persists even now—a neighbourhood in this area flaunts it on the nameplates of a few old houses where descendants of the original residents of Muhammadpuram live today. Ibrahim had called the extension Ibrahimpuram, set up pavilions there and built two artificial lakes that exist even today.

But Ibrahimpuram did not serve its intended purpose. The area was rocky, water was scarce, and the population gathered within the fort spilled out of it. There seemed to be no other option at the time, however. Extending the capital to the east posed a problem because of the Nerva (another name for Musi),[6] a river that 'ran like a brook though in time of the rains, it be as broad as the Seine before the Louvre at Paris,'[7] according to Tavernier. The Nerva, also known as Muchkunda, had its source in the hills of Vikrabad, emerging from a huge pit that resembled a 'gomukh' or the mouth of a cow. This was called a 'kund' and it is possible that the river's old name, Muchkunda, is derived from this, says Anand Raj Varma in his book *Hyderabad—Mohalley, Gali aur Kunche Vol. 1*.

While Ibrahim had contemplated building a new city southeast of the Nerva, he had been unsure of how best to negotiate the river during the rains. Muhammad Quli's romantic escapade had provided the solution.

Before the city of Hyderabad came up, the area that lay south of the river was mostly inhabited by Telugu-speaking people. It was also, at that time, the dwelling of Shah Chirag, a Muslim saint from Najaf. Shah Chirag was in fact the first Muslim to inhabit this locality. While the neighbourhood is now known as Shahalibanda, at that time it was a portion of the predominantly Brahmin settlement, Chinchlam—Bhagmati's village. Here Shah Chirag lies buried according to his last wish. Ironically, Bhagmati's village is also the burial place of Mir Momin Astrabadi—the chief architect of the new city, the prime minister of Sultan Muhammad Quli Qutb Shah and quite possibly the person responsible for Bhagmati's disappearance from the historical record.

The people who lived in what is present-day Shahalibanda came from different cultural backgrounds and economic strata. The place was a centre for various kinds of craft and production activities. Its residents included Hindu and Muslim nobles and military commanders; in fact, it continued to be the foremost site for military establishments as well as for the royal dairy well into the eighteen and nineteenth centuries. Tanners, salt makers, grain carriers, goat sellers, water carriers and torch bearers also lived there as did Muslim talisman makers and faqirs. Islamic tokens or alams were kept in the ashurkhanas there for the commemoration of the ten-day mourning period maintained by Shias for Muharram.

The area also included a neighbourhood of Hindu dancing girls and prostitutes called Nagulachinta. Later, Nagulachinta found a rival in Mahbub ki Mehndi, an area located near Husaini Alam that was famous for Muslim courtesans and musicians.

In later years, the area continued to be as diverse as it ever was, boasting of residents such as military commanders of the Qutb Shahi army, the mostly Hindu serrishtahdars (court administrative officers) including Maharashtrian and Telugu Brahmins, and members of the Kayasth community who worked as record keepers, paymasters and managers of units of troops. Much later, this neighbourhood would produce some of the most famous Hindu poets of Hyderabad.

Muhammad Quli's decision to build the new capital at this spot was a wise one. There was already a road running from Golconda to Masulipatnam—the chief port of the kingdom of Golconda—alongside several coastal towns which would benefit the new city greatly. So when the moon was in the constellation of Leo and Jupiter was in its own mansion (a conjunction the astrologers considered auspicious), Muhammad Quli summoned architects and masons to prepare plans for the new city. Led by Mir Momin, the prime minister, the Persians played an important role in not just drawing up the design and layout of the city but constructing it as well.

Mir Momin, a Sayyid (Sayyids are descendants of the family of the Prophet), had arrived in India in 1581 and found himself a job in Muhammad Quli's court. A scholar, a capable administrator and a deeply religious man, he was first Sultan Muhammad Quli's religious tutor. Their partnership proved to be extremely harmonious and productive.[8] Soon, Mir Momin became the prime minister, an appointment he retained for forty years. He was well versed in Persian, Arabic, divinity, prosody, architecture and weights and measures. Like his emperor, he was a poet and is known to have excelled in the panegyric as well as the lyrical form. Muhammad Quli was impressed and the sultan and the prime minister grew close to each other, with Mir Momin writing qasidas in honour of his king.

Mir Momin was both skilled in and passionate about town planning and the new city offered him the perfect opportunity to exploit his talents. When Quli, with his usual flamboyance, announced that he envisioned a garden city as beautiful as Isfahan but unequalled the world over—a replica of paradise itself—he was greatly influenced by Mir Momin, who had watched the Persian city of Isfahan develop during Shah Abbas' rule.

To build this replica of paradise, Mir Momin recruited the best of workers from Iran: draftsmen such as Mir Abu Talib, Kamal-ud-din Shirazi and Sheheryar Jahan, skilled craftsmen and architects. Finally, in 1591, ten days after Muharram, Muhammad Quli Qutb Shah personally laid the foundation stone of the city on the southern bank of the river Nerva, five miles east of Golconda.

Map of Golconda (Photo courtesy: *Golconda/Bagnagar/ Hyderabad: Rise and Fall of a Global Metropolis in Medieval India* by Serish Nanisetti)

For the design of the city, it was decided that it would be built around a perfectly square building, which would have a minaret on each of its four corners. Each side of the building would face a road: one that led to the Golconda fort, one to Masulipatnam, one to the river, and one in the direction of the Koh-e-toor (Mount Sinai). This central building would have three storeys, and on the roof would be a mosque facing Mecca.

The blueprint Mir Momin had drawn up also showed four arches to be built beyond the central building around a central plaza with a fountain at its centre. Behind the western arch would be the royal palace, stretching across a thousand square metres right up to the river. This area would also house the imperial palace of justice. Beyond the eastern arch, musicians, particularly shehnai players were to be accommodated, as the sultan was very fond of that instrument. The northern and southern arches were to be manned by armed guards. According to Mir Momin, there would be two crosses, one at the Char Minar and the other about two hundred and fifty feet away at the four massive arches of the Char Kaman, with Char-su-ka-Houz (fountain of the four directions) at the centre of it, from which would run four channels, exactly the same as the Garden of Eden. The four channels were to symbolise the heavenly canals of pure water, pure milk, pure honey and pure wine. While the western square would be the dwelling of the sultan himself, the southwestern side would contain his loyal subjects, 'living in eternal submission to the Lord'. On either side of the fountain would be a coconut tree and a betel nut tree, representing Sidr and Talha, the two trees of paradise that would represent the two heavens as in the fifty-sixth chapter of the Quran. Besides these, there would be shops, residences, schools, mosques, inns and a general hospital.

'*Where are the gardens? I want gardens in my dream city*,' the young sultan had asked his prime minister, not knowing the confusion these gardens would create for travellers, scholars and academics later on!

'*There will be twenty-three square kilometres of greenery surrounding two and a half kilometres of the city*,' Mir Momin had replied.

As the plans for the new city were being drawn up, the young sultan had prayed for its future. '*Mera shahr logon sooma moor kar rakhya juntu darya mein man, Ya Sami* (Oh God, fill up my city with people just as you have filled the river with fish).'

But God had other plans. There was an outbreak of cholera (some accounts say the plague) in Golconda. The panicked inhabitants, hoping for divine intervention, fixed a huge taziya or taboot (representation of the tomb of Imam Hussain)[9] in the heart of the city, on Thursday, the first Muharrum of 999 AH. A devout Shia, Muhammad Quli ordered the construction of a building on that spot, designed like the Imam Rosa at Mecca, to protect the city. The building came up as a replica of the taziya. This building eventually became the Charminar, a structure constructed right in the centre of the new city for the cost of 2,00,000 huns[10] or Rs 9 lakh, whereas the four massive arches near it became the Char Kaman. The two crosses, one at the Char Minar and the other about 250 feet away at the four massive arches of the Char Kaman, were meant to represent the two heavens as in the fifty sixth chapter of the Quran, just as Mir Momin had planned.

Professor Batley, the world-renowned architect, says this about the Charminar: 'Deccan proudly wears the Charminar as the best gem upon her zone.'[11] It was money well spent if we are to believe Jean de Thevenot, who has noted that 'there was no edifice in the whole city which appears so splendid to the eye.'[12]

According to historian M.A. Nayeem, since Mir Momin was from Iran and had been tasked by the sultan to build a Safahan-i-Nawi (new Isfahan), the design of the Charminar, with its four towers and four-arched plaza (Char Kaman), had an Iranian antecedent: the Maidān-e Naqsh-e Jahān of Isfahan.[13] However, the construction of the Maidān-e Naqsh-e Jahān (image of the world square) in Isfahan began only in 1598, after the Safavid Shah Abbas (1588–1629) shifted his imperial capital from Qazvin to Isfahan, by which time the Charminar-Char Kaman complex was already being used by Muhammad Quli.

The Charminar was built using granite, lime and mortar and a plaster that included the whites of eggs to give it a smooth and creamy finish. It was constructed at the centre of the new city, and served as the town square or chaubara. Which begs the question: was the Charminar—the city's focal point—built to commemorate the sultan's first meeting with Bhagmati or was it to commemorate the placing of the taziya at that spot by the people of the city? The former reason may be true, but let us not ignore or dismiss the probable intervention of a religious agency in the construction of the edifice. However, assuming that the Charminar was primarily the manifestation of Quli's love for Bhagmati, it serves us well to recall Professor Laura M. Leming's paper titled *Sociological Explorations: What is Religious Agency?*, which explains that agency is not simply action but an action fuelled by memory and a vision for the future. Muhammad Quli, the lover, who built the city for Bhagmati, might have conceived the city as an enduring emblem of their love, possibly imagining a future in which Bhagmati's name would be fondly remembered and her memory cherished.

'*What should we name this magnificent centrepiece?*' the sultan had asked his prime minister.

'*It will be known as the Charminar.*'

Pleased, the sultan had offered a shimmering cloth of gold-coat to Mir Momin and his three assistants. The people of Chinchlam had been given a free meal from the royal kitchen. A slight drizzle had enveloped the new city and this was considered a good omen.

The first buildings that came up in the new city were the Charminar, the Daulatkhana-e-Ali, the Khudadad Mahal, the Jami Masjid, the ashurkhana, the four arches and the fountain. A number of chronograms were prepared once the Charminar was ready. The story behind one of the chronograms is that once a young man called Hasan stepped forward and uttered just two words: Ya Hafiz (an invocation to God as the Protector). There was silence as the audience waited for the rest. By then the master of ceremonies had calculated the numerical value of these two short words and exclaimed that it yielded the year of 1000 AH (1592). Pandemonium broke out and everyone applauded. The sultan placed his hand on the young man's head and offered him a thousand huns and a robe.

The story of the day Quli showed his new city to Bhagmati goes something like this,

After the usual celebrations and protocol, the sultan awaited the arrival of Bhagmati. She arrived in style, with fifty rows of horsemen ahead of her palanquin and fifty rows of horsemen behind it. When she entered the new palace, Quli pulled Bhagmati gently towards the main arch and pointed towards the inscription engraved on it.

'Read!' he said.

'Hyder Mahal!' Bhagmati exclaimed.

Quli smiled. 'That is going to be your new name.' Spreading out his hands, he said, 'For you! This palace and the entire city is your new home. They are yours!'

Tears welled up in Bhagmati's eyes.

'Won't you ask me the name of the city?'

Bhagmati looked at him shyly. 'Tell me.'

'It is named after you. Bhagnagar!'

The grand new city located alongside the unpredictable river was filled with trees, orchards and flowers, creating a dazzling mosaic of colours that impressed all who visited it. Rafiudin Shirazi, who visited the city in 1608, has written in his *Tukftain't Mutuk*, compiled in 1017 AH (1608 CE), that the bazaars and streets were so full of trees that the whole city looked like one big garden sprawling from Nabat Pahad to the Mahal-e-Kohe Toor—just as Muhammad Quli had wanted.

'A large city with magnificent mansions was founded, every one of which had a large garden attached to it. Some of the trees were so tall that they seemed to touch the very sky. The whole city looks like one big garden (bagh), and there is such a variety of fruits from Khurniun and Portugal that they have lost none their worth,' Shirazi has written.

Tavernier, who visited the city nearly fifty years after its foundation, was also much impressed and later remarked that 'the whole city is one large garden'. Throughout his account, Tavernier has referred to the new capital city as Bhagnagar, even half a century after it was built. This is clear from his detailed narrative of Aurangzeb's attack on the kingdom of Golconda when he describes the way the king fled from Bhagnagar to the fortress of Golconda.[14]

There was, however, some confusion about the spelling and pronunciation of Bhagnagar. In most of the reports of contemporary travellers, the new city was either called Bagnagar or Baghnagar (the city of gardens) or Bhagnagar (the city of fortune). Thevenot, who visited the city sixty-five years after it was built, has called it Baghnagar, adding that the official name used for correspondence and government work was Aider-abad.[15] However Ferishta, who lived in the neighbouring kingdom of Bijapur during the reign of Mohammad Quli, has clearly mentioned that the new city was called 'Bhagnuggur, named after the sultan's favourite mistress, Bhagmutty' and that it was only after her death that Quli ordered the name to be changed to Hyderabad. Even so, Hyderabad retained its original name for many years longer.

Muhammad Quli Qutb Shah died in 1612, a year after his beloved Bhagmati passed away as per folklore. (Like everything else about her, Bhagmati's date of death is not certain.) But the city he had built, grew and prospered, throbbing with life. Stories of its wealth and opulence as well as of its rich literary and academic atmosphere had spread across the world and traders and merchants from Iran, Turan, Rome and Syria would bring the choicest goods to satisfy the refined tastes of the people of Golconda, making the streets of the kingdom echo with languages from around the world.

After the deaths of Muhammad Quli and Bhagmati, their daughter Hayat Bakshi Begum became the queen of Golconda. She was married to her cousin Muhammad Qutb Shah, the son of Muhammad Quli Qutb Shah's brother, who became the new sultan. Did Hayat Bakshi Begum know her mother? If she was indeed Bhagmati's daughter, she would have been almost twenty years old at the time of Bhagmati's death, which supposedly happened around 1611. Did Hayat cherish her mother's memory? Or was she made to believe by prime minister Mir Momin and the nobility of the court that Bhagmati was not her mother? Would a queen who was influential across the reigns of three regents as a daughter, a wife and a mother, a woman whose tomb is one of the grandest in the royal necropolis accompanied by the biggest mosque, not want to know her own mother's name? It seems not, because Hayat Bakshi Begum has said not a word about Bhagmati. At least, nothing has been found so far to show that Hayat ever acknowledged being Bhagmati's daughter.

I find that quite surprising considering that Hayat Bakshi was invested with the kind of power that enabled her to intervene successfully on behalf of Abdullah Qutb Shah when Aurangzeb pounded at the kingdom's gates. She was undoubtedly a lady of considerable influence, so why did she remain silent over the fact that her mother's name figured nowhere in the dynasty's records? Wouldn't she have wanted to know why the city where she was born was known as Bhagnagar? Or did she choose to ignore the removal of her mother's name from the family records because she was disinclined to invite the wrath of the nobility and her husband, the new sultan, who apparently had a serious disposition?

Hayat's husband's reign was one of the dynasty's most peaceful. Golconda's neighbours gave no trouble and Aurangzeb had not yet shown up. Unfortunately, Sultan Muhammad Qutb Shah died early, leaving behind his only son, the twelve-year-old Abdullah Qutb Shah, as his heir. The boy had never met his father in all his twelve years of life and therefore, knew nothing of statesmanship. However, Hayat Bakshi, the queen mother or Ma Saheba as she was affectionately called, was still young and took charge of the kingdom. Golconda's situation remained peaceful until Aurangzeb's arrival. Later, when faced with the prospect of Aurangzeb at Golconda's doors, Ma Saheba's clever diplomacy worked and the Mughal prince agreed to restore the kingdom to the Qutb Shahis in return for one crore of rupees as indemnity—the arrears of tribute that had impelled him to invade Golconda in the first place—and the marriage of his daughter with Sultan Abdullah's son. The latter part of the deal was Hayat's master stroke—it kept the Mughals away from Golconda for the next thirty years!

Like her father Muhammad Quli, Hayat Bakshi was smart and preferred to keep her kingdom peaceful. Also like him, she was interested in art and culture and grand buildings. She commissioned a beautiful mosque and a huge sarai or inn in Hayathnagar, an area named after her. The Hayat Bakshi mosque, constructed in 1672 during her son Abdullah Qutb Shah's reign, is a beautiful example of Qutb Shahi architecture and is located on the old route to Masulipatnam. This grand mosque, which was awarded the Intach Heritage award in 2003, was built on a terrace situated within a huge compound. The caravan sarai built around it had a hundred and thirty rooms for the use of weary travellers. Known then as the sarai of Ma Saheba, the building used to have three lofty entrance gates at the north, east and south. Now only the eastern gate is in use.

To the northeast of the mosque is a huge step well called Hathi Ki Baoli, presumably constructed for the animals of the tired travellers. The arches inside it once had bird motifs built into the walls, but it now lies in ruins. Old books of historical value say the mosque had five double arches of massive height and was flanked by two lofty minarets. The prayer niche was made of plaster and bore no inscription.

Perhaps Hayat did not want to stir up conflict in the court regarding her maternity. Her husband's reign was fairly undisturbed, allowing her to spend years in the development of art and architecture. Even so, it is hard to believe that a woman as intelligent as Hayat had no interest in getting to know her lineage from her mother's side. No historical record exists to show that she ever investigated the circumstances of her birth. Assuming she was not Bhagmati's daughter, was she the daughter of Quli's first wife, Mir Shah Mir's daughter, who had been sent away before Bhagmati entered the palace? But Hayat was born in 1592 and Quli's first wife had left the kingdom almost a decade before that. Hayat, it seems, had simply not cared to know who had birthed her. Or, did she know but chose to remain silent?

But we care. We are curious. Who was Hayat's mother? Why did her father have no other children, especially since his only child was a girl? Why would a medieval Muslim ruler have only one wife when his faith as well as his status allowed him more? There are huge gaps in the story that seem unlikely to be bridged any time soon.

Bhagyanagar bhi bolte isku bolte Hyderabad
Mandir, masjid, dharmomajab milko haiteabaad[16]

—Narendra Rai

Muhammad Quli was aware that his nobles and religious ministers were not happy with his decision to name his new city Bhagnagar.

Narendra Luther says in his book *Hyderabad: A Biography* that, 'It was natural that many people became jealous of Bhagmati. Many Persian nobles were not happy with the name Bhagnagar. It was so pagan sounding, they objected ... there were a number of people who harboured ill-will against Bhagmati.'

Because Quli needed their support to maintain a peaceful kingdom, he appeased them with a chronogrammatic epithet—'Farkhunda Buniyad', meaning the fortunate city or 'a city of auspicious foundation', which meant the same thing as Bhagnagar. It was only after Bhagmati's death that the city officially came to be known as Hyderabad, the name suggested by Mir Momin, and this was changed once again, after Aurangzeb sacked the city, to Darul-jihad.

Quli built the new city's first ashurkhana which was commemorated during Muharram. Those who worked there were paid from the royal treasury. Quli paid twelve thousand huns to the needy during Muharram and four lakh huns to the Sayyids and ulemas as well. On the western wall of the ashurkhana was inscribed the name of the reigning sultan—Muhammad Quli. The inner hall, the oldest portion of this building had cost the royal treasury Rs 66,000 to build all those years ago.[17]

Meanwhile, the city of Bhagnagar, boasting of 12,000 mohallas and 14,000 shops, mosques, serais, baths and schools, flourished. The sultan's courtiers competed with each other to build beautiful palaces and gardens within the city that resulted in increased land rents. In turn, the sultan constructed baths and hospitals that were suitably furnished.

Because legend says Muhammad Quli's new city was built to bring his beloved closer to him, it is not surprising that the city became a potpourri of all that is synonymous with love and beauty. As if to match Muhammad Quli's romantic mood, the climate of the region mostly remained perfect. According to French traveller Jean de Thevenot, Bhagnagar was 'a citie that for sweetnesse of ayre, conveniencie of water, and fertility of soyle, is accounted the best situated in India ... [The] rains render the land of this kingdom exceeding fertile, which yields all things in abundance, and especially fruits. Vines are plentiful there and the grapes are ripe in January, though there be some that are not gathered but in February, March or April, according as the vines are exposed to the heat; they make white-wine of them. When the grapes are gathered, they prune the vines, and about midsummer they yield verjuice. In this countrey also they have two crops a year of rice, and many other grains.'[18]

People could take long walks along these gardens, Thevenot has written. They were clean and were sprinkled with fruit, palm and areca trees. The well-gravelled walks were straight and had neat borders of Ghoul Daoudi (a flower that belongs to the chrysanthemum family that in India was known as Gul-i-daudi), as well as other varieties of flowers. Though there were no fountains, the gardens were watered with cisterns and basins. Some gardens, such as the one Thevenot describes, had a canal running through the middle of the walk, carrying water received from small fountains. The magnificent mansions had large gardens attached to them, with very tall trees that almost touched the sky. In *Ma'asir-i-Alamgiri*, Saqi Musta'd Khan has written about Hyderabad: 'The city is like paradise on earth.'

Everything about this new city was impressive and foreign travellers were lavish in their praise of its many attractions. William Methwold, a factor in the East India Company, was in awe of its grandeur, especially that of the palaces, of which there were several. Describing the king's palace, he has said, '... the kings *(sic)* palace, which for bignesse and sumptuousnesse, in the judgement of such as have travelled India, exceedeth all belonging to the Mogull or any other Prince: it being twelve miles in circumference, built all of stone, and, within the most eminent places garnished with massie gold in such things as we commonly use iron, as in barres of windowes, bolts, and such like, and in all other points fitted to the majesty of so great a king, who in elephants and jewels is accounted one of the richest princes of India.' Methwold also describes gates made of ebony and sandalwood, embedded with precious stones, with nails of gold and screens of gold cloths behind the shutters.

The dimensions noted by Methwold could well be exaggerated; the palace described could be the main palace, where the king lived. The city boasted several palaces though—the Dad Mahal, or the palace of justice, the Lalmahal where the royal servants lived, the Jinan Mahal, the Qutb Mandir, the Mahal-e-Kohe Toor, the Aaala Mahal. The grandest was the eight-storey high Khudadad Mahal of which there is an elaborate description in Muhammad Quli's own diwan.

May Khudadad Mahal be blessed by Muhammad
May it be adorned like a replica of heaven
The domes of the Mahal touch the skies
It is adorned with the sun, the moon and the stars
No one in this world has seen such a palace
For it has been brought down to earth by the angels themselves
Its eight balconies are like the eight heavens
The springs of heaven flow through it
Houris, dancers and heavenly maidens
All of them lighter than the breeze, live there
Thanks to the Prophet and the twelve Imams
Enjoy yourself there with your twelve beloveds.

The fifth storey of this grand palace was known as Haider Mahal, the name given to Muhammad Quli's beloved queen Bhagmati.

Muhammad Quli also maintained a manuscript workshop, possibly in the Khudadad palace. All types of book production activities were carried out there, including paper making, manuscript illumination, gilding and painting. The workforce, both local scribes as well as immigrants, were skilled in writing and reading Persian, Arabic and Dakhni.

There are other palaces that Muhammad Quli has mentioned in his diwan—Hira Mahal, Chandan Mahal, Sajjan Mahal and Nadi Mahal. These were his pleasure palaces. Thevenot, who made the effort to measure the size of the capital city, has said that Baghnagar was 5,650 paces in length—2,450 paces from the bridge to the four towers, the Charminar, which formed a kind of town square, and from there through the 'meidan' to the gate were another 3,200 paces.

In his account, Thevenot has mentioned the 'meidan' of Bagnagar, the elephant fights, the palace of Bagnagar, and of course the 'lovely gardens.'[19] He has chronicled the bustling trade process between the Qutb Shahi capital and Masulipatnam: 'They bring from Masulipatan upon Oxen, the Goods which they know to be of readiest sale in Bagnagar ... They are made welcome in that Countrey, because they make many Presents, and a few days before I parted from Bagnagar, their Governour began to have Trumpets and Tymbals, and a Standard carried before him, by Orders from his Superiours.'

This is what Tavernier has to say about the town of Bhagnagar: It was well built, with fine large streets, which were not paved and full of dust and sand. The street that led to the king's palace was very wide. To the right were the houses of nobles and courtiers and four or five two-storeyed caravansarais with large halls and chambers which kept them cool for travellers. At the end of this street, was a large square, adjacent to one of the walls of the palace. In the middle, there was a balcony where the king sat when he wished to grant an audience to his people. The principal door of the palace was not in this square, but in another close by; one first entered a large court surrounded by porticos under which the king's guards were stationed. From this court one passed to another of the same construction, around which there were several beautiful apartments with a terraced roof; upon these, as upon the quarter of the palace where they kept the elephants, were beautiful gardens and such large trees that one wondered how the arches could carry such weight. These elevated gardens were modelled after the gardens of Babylon and were first introduced by the Persians.

Tavernier was either so impressed that he didn't care to check his facts or he was totally confused. He made at least two mistakes in his description of Bhagnagar. The Sultan of Golconda at the time of Tavernier's visit was the incompetent and indolent Abdullah Qutb Shah, Muhammad Quli's grandson, 'who never appeared in public to give audience and administer justice according to the custom of the country, nor did he venture outside the walls of the fortress. Confusion and misrule were the natural and unavoidable consequences of this state of things.'[20] Aurangzeb, in fact wrote to his father Shah Jahan, 'Such a money-yielding country, unmatched by the imperial dominions, has fallen into this wretch's hands.'[21]

Jadunath Sarkar has referred to Golconda's capital city as Haidarabad, while Tavernier, even after half a century of its creation, still called it Bhagnagar. According to Tavernier, Bhagnagar was two kos (about 6 kilometres) distant from the fort of Golconda, which became the residence of Abdullah after he had abandoned his capital, following Aurangzeb's first attack on the sultanate.

The other mistake that Tavernier has made is to refer to Bhagnagar as the town 'commenced by the great grandfather of the king who reigns at present'. However, Abdullah Qutb Shah was the son of Hayat Bakshi Begum who was the daughter of the fifth sultan, Mohammad Quli Qutb Shah, which means Quli was Abdullah's grandfather, not great grandfather. Even if an error of one generation in the royal bloodline can be forgiven, the second blunder Tavernier committed was to assume that Bhagnagar meant 'garden (bagh) of Nagar'—that Nagar was the name of a much beloved wife of Muhammad Quli and the city was named after her! 'He has writen, 'Bhagnagar is then the town which they commonly call Golkonda, and it was commenced by the great grandfather of the King who reigns at present, at the request of one of his wives whom he loved passionately, and whose name was Nagar.' According to Tavernier, the area occupied by the city had earlier been a pleasure resort with beautiful gardens where, on the 'insistence of his beloved wife Nagar', Quli had laid the foundation of a palace and a town he called the Garden of Nagar.

Though Tavernier totally misunderstood the meaning of the name Bhagnagar and got the name of Muhammad Quli's beloved wife entirely wrong, he did understand that the city was built as an edifice of love. Murti writes that Tavernier, with the help of a professional writer, had organised his notes much later, which explains his confusion about Bhagmati's name. The word 'bhag' is similar to the Persian word 'bagh' meaning 'garden' and in accepting that, Tavernier assumed the name of Quli's wife was Nagar.

Tavernier made several trips to the kingdom of Golconda between 1638 and 1663. He may not have met Muhammad Quli but it's likely he met nobles who were alive at the time that the Charminar was built and had witnessed Bhagmati's splendid pageantry move through the streets. It is, therefore, baffling that he got the meaning behind the name of the city so wrong!

Was Muhammad Quli entirely inspired by love, though? It seems unlikely. He cannot be dismissed as just a dreamer, an impulsive youth gripped in the throes of passion. Muhammad Quli was clear about his obligations towards his throne and his faith—the construction of the buildings in general and the erection of the Charminar in particular attest to his loyalty towards both. Both the monument itself as well as the place selected for its construction fit well with Leming's interpretation of agency as action fuelled by memory and a vision for the future.

The building of Hyderabad and especially the Charminar reinforced the Qutb Shahi ideals of a polyvalent religio-cultural climate suitable for the dynasty's political practice of conciliation. In this, the Qutb Shahis deviated from the practices of their Islamic predecessors as well as their contemporaries 'who followed the political practice of desecration, destruction, and reuse of the state deity and royal temple complex.'[22]

No Qutb Shahi architecture, whether religious in nature or not, was a result of destruction, desecration and reuse of Hindu temples. It was, instead, a fusion of the Shiite and Deccani forms of architecture. While Charminar, which was considered the gateway to the new city, was distinctly Shiite, using number symbolism to reinforce the memory of the Shia Imamate and Ahl-e Bait, its design was also influenced by the architectural remains of the erstwhile Kakatiya capital of Warangal that represented early Deccani styles as is evident from the central piazza (the chaubara) and the ceremonial arched gateways (the kirtitorana). In a bid to appease all relevant factions of the population, 'the Qutb Shahis integrated Islamic architecture with local building styles, thus reinforcing the Qutb Shahi identity as both Shia and Deccani; in that the architecture was ostensibly Islamic, yet ambiguous.'[23] This served two purposes: architecture was used as a conciliatory tool by the Qutb Shahis to reach out to the diverse populations over whom they ruled from a minority position, while at the same time the incorporation of the Deccani Indic style into their building designs allowed the Qutb Shahi rulers to assert their religious and political independence from the other Deccan sultanates, the Shiite safavids of Iran and the Sunni Mughals in North India.

The Charminar served as the city square or market square and was the monumental gateway to the new city built by Quli, living up to its original designation as a madarsa. In Persian, madarsa refers to a centrally located place where all necessities of life can be bought.[24] The monument's four minarets marked the four cardinal directions. But this city centre or chaubara is also typical of Deccan architecture, as is evident from similar structures in Bidar seen in Karnataka, Warangal in Telangana and Udgir in Maharashtra. However, instead of having round city markers, the Qutb Shahi capital had arches spanning the road in four directions.[25]

Madarsa also means a school and the first storey of the Charminar was used as one. In fact, the Charminar was the first school started in the Qutb Shahi kingdom and mainly taught Persian and Arabic. With the passage of time, several other madarsas came into being and the original madarsa lost its importance. When teaching was finally stopped at Charminar, the structure was no longer called a madarsa.[26]

The roof of the Charminar was designed after the Mulla Khayalli mosque in Golconda fort that had been constructed by Ibrahim Qutb Shah. On the second storey was a mosque which had a Qibla (prayer niche), five bays, marked spaces to spread the janamaz (prayer mats) and intricate vegetal patterns on its walls. Only forty people could be accommodated at one time. It was probably this mosque that stopped Aurangzeb from destroying the city's stunning centrepiece.

The four minarets of the Charminar each measure a hundred and sixty feet (four storeys) from the plinth to the apex, with large apartments on each landing. There are twelve apartments symbolising the twelve Imams. Along the western side of the rooftop is a mosque with distinctively Shia symbolism. The rooftop prayer hall has five double arches symbolising the panjetan-e-pāk (Muhammad, Ali, Fatimah, Hasan and Husain). The interior gallery is decorated with plaster alam motifs inscribed with the names of Allah, Muhammad and Ali in fine calligraphy. The Qutb Shahi alam[27] design was formalised by 1591 as both an architectural embellishment and a talismanic protection. The alam, in the form of a tear drop, has Sharjah or beastly figures projecting from each side in dramatic relief. These Sharjah, in the form of fierce dragons (azhdaha or makara) with protruding red tongues, are meant to devour evil. In the courtyard at ground level is a fountain primarily intended for ablutions (wuẓū), although it served a dual function as a sabīl as well, providing refreshment to the thirsty in memory of Imam Husain and his companions who suffered from thirst during the battle of Karbala in Iraq in the year 680 CE.

The monument's main building has four impressive arches, one in each direction, each measuring twenty-four by thirty feet, surrounding a small cistern in the centre. Flights of stairs lead to the upper storey and the top portion is double storeyed. The building, made of lime and stone, has fine stucco decorations.

Charminar (Photo courtesy: rawpixel.com)

Some time later, not very far from the Charminar, Muhammad

One of the arches of Char Kaman (Photo courtesy: Shutterstock)

Quli built a piazza of four arches that could serve as passages through which elephants with canopied litters could easily pass, just as Mir Momin had envisioned. The arch or gateway facing west was called the Daulat-Khana-e-Ali (the gate of royal residence) as well as the Sehr-e-Batil Ki Kaman or the Sher Gil Ki Kaman. It had nails of gold and was inlaid with precious stones. In the east was the Naqqar Khana (the palace gate where drums were beaten). The musicians seated there on the top balcony entertained the crowds five times a day. It was later called the Kali Kaman (the black arch) or Kaman of Shambhoo Pershad. In the centre was the Jilau Khana (the royal vestibule). The northern arch facing the river was called the Machli Kaman (the fish arch—a big fish made of bamboo and paper was suspended from the centre of the arch on every lunar new year), fish being a symbol of prosperity and a golden fish being a symbol of high distinction for Muslim nobility and good fortune for the

Qutb Shahis. The arch facing south or Mewe-Walon ki Kaman[28] was originally called Char Minar Kaman, for its nearness to the official entrance of the city's first mosque, the Jami Masjid.

The Qutb Shahi palaces were situated in the direction of the western arch from the time of Muhammad Quli until the last siege of Golconda in 1098 AH. The entrance to the royal palace could be approached after crossing a square thousand-foot courtyard where there stood a huge gate made of sandalwood studded with golden spikes. This was the gate of the royal residence. The adjoining outhouses were used as sitting places for the attendants of the nobles and officials who went every morning to the palace. On either side of the royal gate a few elephants stood by day and night and inside the gate a thousand foot soldiers, two hundred enslaved African men and one thousand horses were drawn up in rank and file, ready for action at any time. The four-cornered octagonal reservoir was meant to quench the thirst of the army.[29]

The southern enclosure housed the privy council chamber, while the northern enclosure, consisting of four apartments, housed the royal wardrobe and other royal offices as well as the soldiers, stewards, clerks on night duty and armour bearers. 'In Chandan Mahal, ordinary armour bearers attended alternately; in Gagan Mahal, Turks, Arabs and Deccani armour bearers used to assemble and the main apartment was reserved for trustworthy servants while Sajan Mahal was set apart for learned and virtuous men,' observes Syed Ali Asgar Bilgrami in his *Landmarks of the Deccan*. In the eastern enclosure was the public dining hall where thousands of men were supplied with delicious food from the royal kitchen both morning and evening.[30]

Highways through each of the four arches mentioned above led to different parts of the city and exactly in the centre of the four arches was the Char-su-ka-hauz, a four cornered reservoir visible from every direction. It is now called Gulzar House. The old terrace that surrounded it was pulled down in 1895 to widen the path and an iron fencing was fixed in its place. The Qutb Shahi kings would sit on the balcony of the royal residence facing this reservoir.

In a contemporary chronicle of the sixteenth century called *Hadiqat-as-Salatin,* Hakim Nizamuddin Gilani called Hyderabad a qita (fragment) of Bihisht (paradise). The city's growth was spectacular right from its inception in terms of area and size, population, economic activities and capacity to meet not just its own needs but those of the surrounding regions as well. It attracted migrants, traders and all kinds of professionals from all over the world and was considered 'the centre of all trade in the east'. It was a large, spacious and thickly populated city. According to several travellers, the Qutb Shahis not only patronised local traders, handicrafts and industries, but also imported merchandise from the coastal region of Deccan, the gulf countries and Persia. The Telugu-speaking merchants formed a large section of the traders and offered stiff competition to the Persians. Masulipatnam was Hyderabad's chief trading post in the east, but the city was also very well-connected with Goa, Surat and the Malabar coast in the west.

Muhammad Quli allowed a lot of liberty to his subjects as is clear from Thevenot's account of the status of women, both prostitutes, whom he calls public women, as well as married women: 'Publick women are allowed in the kingdom, so that no body minds it when they see a man go to their houses, and they are often at their doors well drest, to draw in passengers. But they say most of them are spoiled. The common people give their wives great liberty. When a man is to be married, the father and mother of his bride make him promise that he will not take it ill that his wife go and walk through the town, or visit her neighbours, nay and drink tary, a drink that the Indians of Golconda are extremely fond of.' Polygamy, though permitted, was not generally practised.[31]

According to *A Short History of Aurangzib* by historian Jadunath Sarkar, during Abdullah's reign, Hyderabad had twenty thousand public women or courtesans and countless taverns 'where 1,200 large leather bottles of fermented palm-juice were consumed daily'. Abul Hasan, Abdullah's successor, left matters of the state to his Hindu prime minister Madanna and shut himself in his palace with a host of concubines and dancing girls. When Aurangzeb's army came galloping into Hyderabad, Abul Hasan[32] fled the capital city to seek refuge in the Golconda fortress while the Mughal emperor's army razed the city that Muhammad Quli had so lovingly built for his wife Bhagmati.

Khafi Khan—having witnessed the general demoralisation of Hyderabad during Aurangzeb's siege of Golconda and the presence of the Mughal army in the area for long stretches of time—in his book *Muntakhab-al Lubab*, links Bhagmati's name with the establishment of numerous brothel houses and taverns in Bhagnagar and Golconda at the time. This confusion probably arose because Bhagmati was believed to be from the Bhogam caste. Though Khafi Khan traces the foundation of Bhagnagar to the Quli-Bhagmati love story, even calling Bhagmati the sultan's wife, he writes: 'That Woman had established many brothels and drinking shops in that place, and the rulers had always been addicted to pleasure and all sorts of debauchery ... so the city got an evil name for licentiousness.'

In Bhagmati, they found a handy scapegoat. This was typical of all the Mughal chroniclers whose unsympathetic attitude towards Bhagmati reflected the socio-religious taboos against the Bhogamwars. Tavernier however clarifies in his own way that Bhagmati had no role to play in the decadence of the city. It was the intoxicating drink, tari, that was the cause for the city's decadence, its consumption of alcohol and the resultant excise duty collected that kept the royal exchequer tingling.[33]

The Qutb Shahi rulers gave religious freedom to both Hindus and Muslims. Members of both communities could attain the highest offices in the state. In some respects, the knowledge and skill of the Brahmins made them indispensable to the administration, because while they were employed to write and keep accounts on palm leaves with pens of iron, they were also competent astronomers, observing the course of the seven planets. In fact, the first ten days of Muharram were held sacred not only by the Muslims—both Shias and Sunnis—but also by the Hindus.

In my opinion, Muhammad Quli built Bhagnagar for practical reasons but named it after Bhagmati out of love. After Bhagmati married Quli, she was bestowed with the title of Haider Mahal by her husband who, in order to make his prime minister and the orthodox nobility happy, then called the city Hyderabad. This meant the city was named after both his queen and Ali. For a while, the city was called both Bhagnagar and Hyderabad—the latter for official purposes. However, the unofficial name of the city stuck for a long, long time as can be seen in various texts and maps written and drawn by both locals and travellers.

Sultan Muhammad Qutb Shah, Quli's nephew and successor, commissioned a work called *Tarikh-i-Muhammad Qutb Shahi (TIQS)*. The work is accepted as an authentic history of the Qutb Shah dynasty from its beginning until 1616. Murti writes that though *TIQS*, which was completed in 1617, gives a fairly detailed description of the beginnings of Hyderabad as well as the circumstances that led to its foundation, there is no mention of either Bhagmati or Bhagnagar in the chronicle. This annoyed Murti who quotes Prof. Abdul Majeed Siddiqui on the matter: 'The author of the Qutb Shahi, the chief source of the Qutb Shahi history, is silent on the point. His silence makes the matter all the more doubtful.'

This silence, according to Murti, was manipulated by disbelievers of the legend to show that the story of Bhagmati was a 'fabrication of the ill-informed contemporary gossip-mongering writers, perpetuated by the romance-loving Asaf Jahi chroniclers'. Court chroniclers were usually panegyrists who chose not to allude to embarrassing statements and unpleasant episodes since they wanted to stay alive. 'The Muslim chroniclers usually chose to avoid any mention of the names of ladies of the harem unless it was compulsory for their narratives, and more so if they were involved in any scandalous controversies,' Murti remarked. At the same time, it must be noted that the story of Bhagmati was neither condemned nor denied in *TIQS*, though the writer of the chronicle did have both earlier and more contemporary works at his disposal, definitely those of Nizamuddin Ahmed and Ferishta and possibly the work of Faizi, all of which mentioned the 'scandalous' episode of Bhagmati.

It's even possible that the chronicler had heard the rumours firsthand, since at the time *TIQS* was written, it had been only five years since Muhammad Quli's death and twenty-five years since the city was founded. Thus, says Murti, 'if the official history did not refer to the episode of Bhagmati, which had attained celebrity or notoriety depending on the view point, from Deccan to Hindustan, through Bijapur, Ahmadnagar, Lahore and Agra, it should be only logical to consider it as a deliberate act of self-censorship on the part of the discreet author or one imposed by the ruling clique that acted as the conscience-keeper of the kingdom, instead of treating it as a figment of imagination that misdirected the judgement of the well-established contemporary historians who created the episode out of nothing for the sheer pleasure of it.'[34]

In his book *Golconda/Bagnagar/Hyderabad: Rise and Fall of a Global Metropolis in Medieval India,* Serish Nanisetti quotes Francois Martin, the first Governor-General of Pondicherry, also known as the father of Puducherry, to make a point about the name of the city. Martin, who reached the Deccan region in 1670, has mentioned the word 'Bagnagar' twenty-seven times in his book *Memoires de Francois Martin, Fondateur de Pondicherry* (1665-1696). If the city's name had really been the figment of someone's imagination, it should have been erased by the time this book was written. What is also interesting is Martin mentioning that, while resting at Assenbole on the way from Madras to Bagnagar, he had met a troupe of dancing girls on their way back from the royal festival that was held once a year to serve as a reunion for all those who belonged to the caste of dancing women. In fact, about twelve thousand dancing women had attended the festival at the capital when Martin met them.[35] This proves the authenticity of various contemporary reports that talk of such a festival being conducted in memory of Bhagmati.

The Descriptive Catalogue of Historical MSS (1854), compiled by William H. Morley, a trustee of the Royal Asiatic Society of Great Britain and Ireland, also mentions Bhagnagar.[36] But this could have been Morley's own addition to the text as he might have been familiar with the name Bhagnagar, says Murti. The actual manuscript may not have contained the name Bhagnagar at all.

In his map titled *Penisola Dell India di Qua Dal Gange*, the Italian cartographer Giacomo Cantellida Vignola has mentioned both Bagnagar and Golconda, but has made no reference to Hyderabad. The map was created in Rome in 1683, nearly ninety years after the foundation of Quli's new city. *Empire de Mogul*, the 1688 map by Robert Morden, also names Bagnagar and Golconda as navigation points.

After a posting in Hyderabad, Daniel Havart of the Dutch East India company left behind a detailed map of the Golconda fort and the annex and called it naya qila (new fort)—built after 1656. While identifying the various entrances to the fort, he identifies the main entrance as Bagnagar Darwaza, which opened to the road leading to the new city built to the east of the fort. As per Havart, after Aurangzeb conquered Golconda, the name of Bagnagar Darwaza was changed to Fateh Darwaza.[37]

Tavernier made five trips to Golconda and has mapped out a 'Route de Benares a Bagnagar (route from Benares to Bagnagar)'. In his memoirs, he has written that Bhagnagar was the town vulgarly called Golconda.

We also have a story of Bhagmati and Bhagnagar (unnoticed by Sherwani) from a later Mughal chronicle called *Masir-i-Alamgiri (Memories of Aurangzeb)* by Saqi Mustad Khan, who had been present at Golconda during its siege in 1687 by Aurangzeb. Khan was officially commissioned to write the chronicle soon after the death of Aurangzeb as a sequel to the *Alamgir Nama*. 'The city of Haidarabad is situated two kos from the fort of Golconda; it was founded by Muhammad Quli Qutbul Mulk, who was infatuated by the courtesan Bhagmati. Afterwards it got its present name,' Mustad Khan has written in the *Masir-i-Alamgiri*.

Another reference to Bhagnagar can be found in French traveller, priest and writer Abbe Carre's book *The Travels of the*

Abbe Carre in India and the Near East, where he has said that he had been the guest, for five or six days, of a Capuchian monk at the Portuguese Church at Millapur (Gudi Malkapur), which was between 'Bhagnagar and Golconda.'[38]

A reference to the diocese of Hyderabad-Deccan in the Catholic Encyclopaedia published in 1907 states that Hyderabad was also called Bhagnagar and Farkhunda Buniyad.[39]

In his book *Travels in the Mogul Empire 1656-1668,* French physician and traveller Francois Bernier has quoted from a letter sent by Mir Jemla, the wazir of Golconda, to the Mughal prince Aurangzeb, in which the wazir has said, 'The body of horse is escorting an ambassador from Chah-Jehan, who has affairs of moment to negotiate with the king at Bagnageur.'[40]

In the *Antiquities of Bidar (1944),* Dr Ghulam Yazdani, writes: 'Ali Barid Shah died in 1579 ... he was expelled in 1601 by Mirza Ali Barid, another member of the family, and compelled to fly to Bhagnagar.'

Aziz Ahmad writes in *An Intellectual History of Islam in India,* 'At Golconda, one of the rulers, Sultan Muhammad Quli Qutb Shah, was himself a poet of unique genius. Artistic to the core, he founded the city of Bhagnagar, later known as Hyderabad, as a gesture of his love for his Hindu courtesan Bhagmati.'

The English traveller Isabel Burton who visited Hyderabad in 1879 has written, '... We must remember that Hyderabad is not an ancient city. It owes its origin to Sultan Muhammad Quli ... who built a country palace for one of his mistresses, the lady Bhagwati (not Bhagamuttee), a Hindu of no particular caste; and after assigning to her a guard of a 1,000 horsemen, called the outpost Bhagnagar.'[41]

A Golconda miniature painting entitled *Animals and Ascetics in a Landscape,* which is now in the G.W. Gemmell Collection,

Suffolk, carries on it a handwritten endorsement: 'Bought at Bhagnaggr, purchase price 800 rupees, checked today in 1690.' A painting in the Salar Jung Museum dated 1680 has the word Bhagnagar prominently inscribed on the reverse in what is called Rajasthani Hindi.

The Islamic Culture, an English language Islamic quarterly magazine published in 1943 by the government of the Nizam of Hyderabad, quotes several historical references that seem to prove the existence of Hyderabad city's original name. For example, the magazine states that one Muhammad Zahid Beg, who had copied Mirza Beg's book *Yusuf Zulaikha*, ascribed the date and place at the end of his work as follows: 'On Monday the 24th Dhu'l-Hajja, year 1067 AH [1656] in the city of Bhagnagar.'[42] It also quotes the Muslim historian Khwajah Nizamuddin Ahmad who had written the following in *Tabaqat-i-Akbari* in 1003 AH (1592): 'Muhammad Quli succeeded his father. He became the lover of a prostitute of the name Bhagmati and having laid the foundation of a city called it Bhagnagar. He had 1,000 horsemen as the retainers of that woman. He is ruling the country to the present day, which is in the year 1002 AH and in the 38th year of the Ilahi era, for nine years.'[43]

Next, *The Islamic Culture* quotes from Ferishta's *Tarikh-i-Firishta*: 'In the year 998 AH, the king determined to remove the seat of government on account of the congested situation in Golconda, which from many causes particularly the want of water, became extremely unhealthy, he accordingly fixed on a spot situated at a distance of five kos from its former capital on the banks of the river Moosy, where he laid the foundation of a new city, which he called Bhagnagar (after his favourite mistress); but after her death he ordered it to be called Hyderabad, although for many years it retained its original name.'[44]

Finally, *The Islamic Culture* quotes from *Muntakhab-al Lubab,* the work of Muhammad Hashim: 'He [Muhammad Quli] had a wife named Bhagmati whom he loved the most. At her request he laid the foundation of a city two kos from the fortress of Golconda so he named it after her. Sometime after the death of Bhagmati this name changed to Hyderabad, but the public still calls it Bhagnagar.'[45]

In an earlier edition (April 1934) of *The Islamic Culture,* Professor Rai Bahadur Surya Kumar Bhuyan's translation of a letter written by the Mughal emperor Shah Jahan to the Adil Shahi sultan is mentioned. In one part of the letter, Shah Jahan refers to Bhagnagar: 'It is extremely improper that the rulers of the dominions of Bijapur, Golconda and Bhagnagar situated on the sea have been circulating gajmohurs or independent coins in their realms ...'[46]

Among the later chroniclers of the Asaf Jahi period, those who kept alive the traditional romance of Quli and Bhagmati are Munim Khan Hamdani (*Sawanih-i-Dakan,* 1776), Abu Turab Shustari (*Hadiqatul Alam,* 1799), Ghulam Hussain Khan (*Gulzar-e Asafiyah,* 1844) and Ratanlal Sarmast (*Tuhfa-e-Dakan,* 1862). Of all the Persian chronicles, both Mughal and Deccani, only the *Mah Nama* (History of Chanda Bai Mahalaqa, 1810) of Ghulam Hussain Khan Jauhar has vehemently dismissed the Bhagmati legend.

Even in 1951, Bhagnagar received its due for being the original name of Hyderabad city. Speaking at the inaugural session of the 14th Indian Political Science Conference at the Arts College Hall of Osmania University, the then vice chancellor Nawab Ali Yawar Jung Bahadur said: 'Many of you are visiting Hyderabad and this university presumably for the first time. It is in many ways a beautiful city with a fascinating history. Founded in 1589 by Muhammad Quli, it was originally named Bhagnagar.'[47]

With so many historical and modern references so easily discovered, it seems clear that the original name of Hyderabad was Bhagnagar and not Bagnagar, says the Hyderabad-based history scholar and journalist S. Umamaheshwar in his paper *Bhagnagar, Bhagyanagar or Hyderabad*. He adds that the word 'Bhag' is a corruption of the Sanskrit word 'Bhagya', which means prosperity, affluence and happiness, good fortune, luck and fate.

Whatever the city was called, whether Bhagnagar, Bagnagar, Baghnagar, Bhagyanagar, Shahr-e-Haider, Haider Nagar or Hyderabad, it undoubtedly became the grand city that its founder had dreamed it would be.

CHAPTER 4

Whispering Graves

Pyar se aankh bhar aati hai kanwal khilte hain;
Jab kabhi lab pe tera naam-e-wafaa ata hai.

—Makhdoom Mohiuddin

There is no material evidence that Bhagmati existed. And even if she did exist, she has been erased from history. So why do poets still offer paeans to her? Why do historians and scholars still debate her historical presence? Why do artistes across genres still dedicate their art to her and celebrate the love story of Muhammad Quli and Bhagmati? Why is it that even four hundred years after her passing, the people of Hyderabad still remember her name?

Historians ask predictable questions. Who was Bhagmati? What is the proof that she existed? If she is not mentioned in the dynasty's hagiography, if there are no coins, no inscriptions, not even a grave as evidence of her existence, did she ever exist?

Fair enough. No proof, no queen. Despite this, Bhagmati is a part of Hyderabad's story. Queens have come and gone, but is any consort or wife or queen of any other Qutb Shahi ruler more famous than Bhagmati? Isn't it ironic that the queen who is said to not have existed is the most famous queen of the dynasty? Even Hayat Bakshi Begum (Ma Saheba), who is much loved by the people of Hyderabad, is not as popular as Bhagmati.

Damnatio memoriae, a modern Latin phrase, perhaps explains Bhagmati's case the best. Its dictionary meaning is 'condemnation of memory' or historical negation: per the Oxford English Dictionary, a deceased public figure identified as an enemy of the state was erased from public record, typically by obliterating inscriptions, destroying statues or portraits, or revoking measures introduced by that person and consignment to obscurity. There are and have been many ways to damnatio memoriae—through the destruction of depictions in art, the removal of names from inscriptions and documents, large-scale rewriting of history and even the removal of graves. There is nothing new about damnatio memoriae. Powerful vested interests almost always get their way. But while there is no mention of Bhagmati in any official record, when a story is believed by so many people for more than four centuries, it is likely to be true, says Narendra Luther, author, columnist and an authority on Hyderabad. Besides, '[i]t is romantic and fits in with the temperament of the prince and is in tune with the spirit of the time,' Luther says in his book *Prince, Poet, Lover, Builder: Muhammad Quli Qutb Shah, the Founder of Hyderabad*.

In fact, the very act of trying to relegate Bhagmati to oblivion has kept her name alive. So where does history end and legend begin? To answer this question, I needed to return to the Charminar and Muhammad Quli's city—now known as the old city of Hyderabad.

You won't see me anywhere. But I'm here, near that shop, behind that house. Can't you see me on the first floor of the Charminar? I walk the streets here, I am in the heart of every resident of this neighbourhood. But most of all, I am in my master's heart. He built this city for me, for us. My master lies in his grave a little towards the west. He wanted me to rest beside him there but I told him to allow me to rest in my village. In any case, they would have dug up my grave and exhumed my remains to hide the proof of my existence.

Have you not seen my village? It was here that my master came to see me every day. When I first saw him he was a mere boy riding a horse, his head held high. I was on my way to offer oil and flowers at the temple. He blocked my way and stared at me. Then he said he would send his men to take me to his palace. At first, I was terrified. Had I done something wrong? I had never even seen the royal palace on the other side of the river! He went away that day, but returned every day. I told my mother and grandmother about him. They trained me in singing and dancing. My grandmother smiled and said it was time for me to present a mujra in the royal palace. Because the man who had accosted me was perhaps a prince.

It was the month of Ramzan once again. I like to visit the old city at this time of the year, preferably after dark. But now it was quite late. The lights had gone off and the stars were out. There was an eerie silence. Under this star-spangled canopy lay a story hidden in the crevices of Telangana's rocky landscape, a story that the world needed to be told.

The city would soon wake up, the devout hurriedly preparing the one meal they would eat until after sunset. I left reluctantly, eager to return the next evening and keen to spend the afternoon before that reading *Romance of Kings and Commoners in Golcunda,* Dr Rahimuddin Kemal's story of Bhagmati, a woman whose voice has been muffled, whose spirit has been crushed beneath the burden of politics, governance, religion, class and caste for four centuries. Bhagmati will not be found in history books. But it is important to seek her voice because she is so much a part of the city's identity. In writing her story, Dr Kemal allowed Bhagmati to speak and this is what she says about Quli's love for her:

When news of our love spread, my master was confined in the palace in Golconda. His father, the sultan, wanted him to forget me. Weeks passed and we did not see each other. Then one night, it rained heavily. The river rose, washing away villages on its northern bank, submerging others. My village was about to go under too and we rushed to the upper storey of our house, which had a terrace.

Then I heard something. Hooves splashing through water. A lone rider galloped towards our house. My master had broken through the security of his palace and crossed the river to find me. What if he had died while crossing the river?

He hugged me tightly. Thank Allah you are safe, he said again and again. We spent the whole night holding each other. I will come back to take you to my palace, he reassured me as he left. In the next few days, his father, the sultan, ordered a bridge to be built over the river. Months later, I began visiting my master in his palace, accompanied by a thousand cavalrymen under the command of a Turkish officer, designated by my master to protect me. But our happiness was short lived.

The sultan died and Queen Mother Bhagirathi and the noble Raya Rao manoeuvred to put my master on the throne. After that, my master married prime minister Mir Shah Mir's daughter. My master told me he had been forced to marry her even though she had been betrothed to his brother, Shah Abdul Qader. When prime minister Mir Shah Mir was away in Naldurg, some nobles got the Deccanis to support my master. The Deccanis were angry anyway since the heir apparent, Shah Abdul Qader, lovingly called Shah Sahib, was a Sunni, while Shah Mir's daughter was a Shia. So my master had to marry Shah Mir's daughter for political reasons, to win the support of these foreigners against the Sunni nobles and mashaiks of Gulbarga.

Even though my master married Shah Mir's daughter, he gave me the title of Qutb Mushtari so I would know he hadn't forgotten me. He also asked me to move into Daulat Khana-e-Ali. My master's wife became the queen of Golconda, but not for long. When the prime minister returned from Naldurg, my master asked him to leave the kingdom along with his daughter.

These streets, these mohallas, these shops that you see around you were built by my master. He hired the best architects from Persia. This city was a symbol of our love. My master said he named it after me. Not Queen Bhagirathi, your mother? I asked. No, he said. I named it for you.

But the nobles weren't happy. I was too lowborn to be his beloved, they thought. When my master asked the court poet Mulla Wajhi to write a ballad on our love, Wajhi presented Qutb Mushtari, a wonderful masnawi in which Mushtari was a dancing girl from Chinchlam. But Mir Momin rewrote it. Mushtari was no longer a dancing girl from Chinchlam. Instead, she was a princess from Bengal. For how could the sultan have a courtesan as a wife and queen?

After this, Mir Momin became more and more powerful. He appointed his own men in high posts without even consulting my master. When he began to have the names of Iranian emperors read in the Khutbah, it was said that he was trying to make Golconda a subordinate kingdom of Persia.

My mother worried about me. She thought the Persians in the court wanted to eliminate me since my presence there gave the Deccani people access to my master.

Dr Kemal also gives voice to Bhagmati's sadness at her daughter being snatched away from her:

When I told my mother I was carrying a child, she told me she wanted my confinement to be in my village, with her. My master was so delighted on learning that I was pregnant that he said he planned to marry me and even composed a jalwa (marriage song) for the occasion. But when my daughter was born, Mir Momin took her away from me, denying me the right to bring up my own child. My master continued to visit me, but as time passed, his visits became infrequent.

This is what Bhagmati has to say—in Dr Kemal's words—about the new city being named after her:

Then one day, he told me he had built a palace for me in the new city. By then, I was so sad that I had lost interest in life. In any case, the plague broke out so the Charminar was erected as a taziya to ward off evil. Mir Momin suggested that the new city be called Hyderabad, after Hazrat Ali's son-in-law Haider, to give it piety and dignity. The sultan knew what Mir Momin had in mind. So he called the officer of records and said that Mushtari—that is I—must now be honoured by the title of Hyder Mahal; that the palace built for me would be known as Hyder mahal or Hydermandwa and that the city of Bhagnagar would be called Hyderabad. He also wrote a poem in which he said the bud of Bhag blossomed and was begotten of a life-sustaining daughter called Hayat Baksh. The poem was sent to the calligraphers' workshop, from where it never emerged again.

Bhagnagar. Hyderabad. This city was supposed to be a symbol of my master's love for me. Instead, I lost everything. My daughter. My name. My very existence. Historians were commissioned to write the history of Golconda and its king Quli Qutb Shah without reference to me. My daughter believed she had a Persian mother. The nobles even conspired to marry her to someone from a land far from Golconda so she would hear no more of her mother. Fortunately, my master, who was fond of his nephew Sultan Mirza (Mohammad Qutb Shah) and had declared him as his successor, decided to marry our daughter to him.

Mir Sahib punished me for my existence. He removed my name from all records forever for the interest of the state and the prestige of the sovereign. Only time will tell them that my love and devotion for my master did not deserve punishment.

Until the end of the seventeenth century, Hyderabad was commonly called Bhagnagar, though the spelling of the name was corrupted. Foreigners, especially European travellers, often mispronounced and misspelt Indian names. For example, the Frenchman Thevenot missed the 'H' in Hyderabad and in Bhagnagar, calling the city 'Aiderabad' and 'Bagnagar'. In 1614, Peter Floris, a Dutch trader working for the East India Company in Masulipatnam, wrote to his colleague Tho. Aldworth in Surat, '... this John coming from Barampur towards Bagnagar was robbed by the way by his own report of a camel, a horse ... He came to Bagnagar where he did meet with a certain gentile, being a goldsmith, an old acquaintance of mine.' Qutb Shah became Cotebixa, Pulicat became Paleacattee and Mir Jumla became Mir Sumela in Floris' writings.

Meanwhile, Pieter Gielisz van Ravesteyn, who served in the Dutch trading post at Masulipatnam between 1608 and 1614, has referred to the capital city only as Bagnagar and not as Golconda or Hyderabad,[1] while English merchant William Finch has mentioned Bhagnagar, but written it as Braganadar, as early as 20 July 1609 in his memoirs of his tour of India between

1608 and 1611. While describing a battle between the Mughals and the Deccan sultanates, Finch writes: 'Sha Selim commanded [his troops] ... to invade all the kingdoms from hence to South, even to Cape Comorin, for which a large army was assembling in resistance of whom three great kings were combined, the king of Deccan (Ahmednagar), the king of Visapor (Bijapur), and the king of Golconda(whose chiefe citie is Braganadar), who also gathered forces ...'[2]

In 1622, Heinrich von Poser, a German traveller from Silesia, wrote that he had arrived at the city of Bagnagar, where the ruler was Muhammad Qutb Shah. 'On 3rd (3 December 1622) we reached the city of Bagneger or Hederabat, the capital of the realm and the seat of Sultan Mehemet Culi Cuttub Shah.'[3]

Only around the late seventeenth century, after the Mughal conquest of Hyderabad in 1686 or perhaps even later, did the name Bhagnagar seem to fall out of favour. Thereafter, all correspondence, firmans and records as well as contemporary accounts of travellers and official chronicles mention the city of Hyderabad, not Bhagnagar. Even so, as late as 1816, after the East India Company had spread across India, the cartographer Aaron Arrowsmith created a huge map in which two landmarks were named Hyderabad and Bagnagar.

After Aurangzeb's death in 1707, Hyderabad acquired a new set of rulers—the Asaf Jahs, better known as the Nizams of Hyderabad. The Asaf Jahs were originally administrators who ruled the Golconda sultanate on behalf of successive Mughal emperors until 1724, after which Asaf Jah I established autonomy over the Deccan province and named the region Hyderabad Deccan though he still flew the Mughal flag. For the next one hundred and thirty years, until India's first war of Independence in 1857 and even after that until the turn of the century, Hyderabad remained one of India's richest states. The last Nizam of the state of Hyderabad, Mir Osman Ali Khan, crowned in 1911, was known to have been the wealthiest man in the world in his time. In its 22 February 1937 issue, *Time* magazine, featured him on its cover as 'The Richest Man in the World'. The Nizam's personal fortune was estimated to be roughly £110 million and included £40 million in gold and jewels, a Rs 1,000 crore diamond that he used as a paperweight and a collection of 50 Rolls-Royce cars. His net worth was over $200 billion. At the time of India's independence, Hyderabad was the largest princely state in India in terms of both population and gross national product; it had its own currency, radio broadcasting network, airline, mint, railways and postal system.

The Nizams could well be thankful to Muhammad Quli for their wealth, because he had earnestly prayed for abundance and prosperity for his new city, which he had called Bhagnagar. In some instances, the city is also referred to as Bhagyanagar—the city of fortune. (The word 'fortune' in Telugu is 'Bhagyamu' and in Sanskrit, 'Bhagya'.) Even if we assume the city was named after Bhagmati, its chronogrammatic epithet was 'Farkhunda Buniyad' or 'the fortunate city', which means the same as Bhagyanagar. Clearly, much lies in a name!

The city seemed to be blessed as much by Muhammad Quli's prayers as by his munificence that attracted not just adventurers and kings from across the world, but even the gods. It is believed that Lakshmi, the goddess of fortune and wealth, chose to dwell in Hyderabad because she was impressed by Muhammad Quli's generosity. The story goes that when the end of the Qutb Shahi dynasty neared, the goddess decided to leave the city. As she approached the gates of the kingdom, she was stopped by a guard who was shocked to see a beautiful lady dressed in fine attire and jewellery out alone at night. At his insistence, the goddess revealed her true self. Fearing that with her exit the kingdom would lose its good fortune, the guard asked her to wait while he informed his superiors that she was about to leave and made her promise that she would remain there until he returned.

After informing Tana Shah, the last Qutb Shahi sultan, about the situation, the guard begged to be executed because if he died and never returned to the gate, the goddess would never be able to leave the city. When the king refused to have him killed, the guard jumped to his death. Goddess Lakshmi was thus left within the city, bound by her promise to remain there until the guard returned.

For about two hundred and fifty years after the Qutb Shahi rule ended, little or no mention could be found in any official records of a city called Bhagnagar. However, the legend persisted. Travellers continued to write about Muhammad Quli's splendid city built for his lover Bhagmati. Romantic legends seldom die, especially if, like the story of Hyderabad, they are backed by a symbolic manifestation that survives centuries of assaults perpetrated by both nature and man. But in the twentieth century, the legend of Bhagmati was well and truly dusted off and brought back to the land of the living as a symbol of Deccani identity. Dr Syed Mohiuddin Qadri Zore, a poet and scholar, was the man who revived the legend. This was because Hindustani migrants from the north of India, who had started arriving in Hyderabad after the 1857 uprising . They began occupying key posts in state administration and infringing on patronage for the local culture, thus triggering a north-south conflict. When, after the exit of the last Mughal emperor Bahadur Shah Zafar, the Asaf Jah dynasty tried to claim an imperial legacy, the people of Hyderabad became resentful. For them, the idea of replacing the

Qutb Shahi legacy that they so dearly cherished with some other cultural identity was unacceptable.

Dr Zore took it upon himself to revive the Qutb Shahi Deccani culture. First, he edited the poetic works of Muhammad Quli, proclaiming him the first published Urdu poet and preserving the works in the Idara-e-Adbiyat-e-Urdu, an institution he founded. Next, he initiated an exhaustive study of the Deccan and urged his contemporaries to examine Dakhni texts for fresh perspectives on the region's history. Prodded by Zore, scholar Abdul Majeed Siddiqui completed his *History of Golconda*. Salar Jung III, the prime minister of Hyderabad, sponsored the publication of various Dakhni manuscripts. Meanwhile Zore himself began documenting the myths and legends that formed an integral part of Hyderabadi culture. Of these, the most popular were, of course, about the love story of Muhammad Quli and Bhagmati.

However, historian and scholar Haroon Khan Sherwani was not pleased by Zore's efforts. For Sherwani, Bhagmati was just a myth and as such, could not be allowed into the haloed precincts of academia. By refusing to acknowledge Bhagmati's existence, Sherwani tried to deny the people of Telangana the right to own their history and take pride in it. This led to something of a war between intellectuals, with several other scholars backing Zore even as the people of Hyderabad and Sherwani's own students accused the dissenting historian of being khatta (sour)!

The controversy brought Bhagmati back into the spotlight and Sherwani has himself devoted nearly twelve pages to her in his book *Muhammad-Quli Qutb Shah: Founder of Haidarabad*—probably more than any other record keeper or contemporary chronicler ever did—in his attempt to dismiss the existence of the dancer and her role in the sultan's life!

In fact, Sherwani begins his chapter on Bhagmati by acknowledging exactly what he himself was trying to dismiss: that the story of Bhagmati, whether true or not, has been told for centuries. 'There is a problem in connection with the founding of the City of Haidarabad which has so far remained unsolved,' Sherwani wrote. 'Its importance is due not so much to its intrinsic merit as to its *persistence* since the beginning of the eighteenth century.'

This is exactly the point. When a story continues to be told through generations, especially if it is aligned with the intrinsic spirit of a place, it can be neither ignored nor changed. The love between one of Hyderabad's most beloved rulers and a dancer is cherished by the people of the city because it holds the very soul of Hyderabadi culture. When pedagogues insist on demanding evidence for the story, they miss the overriding narrative that the people have chosen to believe, preserve and cherish.

All representations of the love story in popular culture resonate with the city's heart and soul and echo the collective voice of its people. The H.K. Sherwani Centre for Deccan Studies at the Maulana Azad National Urdu University once even hosted *Quli Dilon Ka Shahzaada*—a dance drama based on the love story of Muhammad Quli and Bhagmati, complete with qawwali and nazms in Urdu and Persian that had been composed by Muhammad Quli himself. Produced and directed by the theatre personality Mohammed Ali Baig in February 2014, the play was well received by an appreciative audience and has become a staple of the Qadar Ali Baig Theatre Foundation's repertoire. The esteemed Professor Khatta must have rolled in his grave!

Sherwani blames Faizi, the brother of Abul Fazl, the trusted minister of Mughal emperor Akbar, for generating interest in the alleged love affair of the sultan and the dancer and thus, keeping scholars and historians across centuries busy trying to either prove or deny Bhagmati's existence. The passage written by Faizi that kindled the controversy says: 'Ahmad Quli *(sic)* is steeped in Shi'ism, and has built a city Bhagnagar by name, after Bhagmati, the old prostitute (fahisha-i-kuhna) who has been his mistress for a long time (ma'shuqa-i Qadim).'

Faizi was the Mughal envoy to the Deccan from 1591 to 1594 and he had mentioned Bhagmati in his letter to Akbar, referring to the sultan in a condescending manner. But Faizi was connected to the Mughals who were Sunnis while the Qutb Shahi rulers were Shias, which explains the snobbery and sense of superiority. Besides, politically, the Mughals didn't consider the Deccan sultans as kings of any exalted stature.

But Sherwani rejects what Faizi writes in this letter, calling it 'wholly inaccurate'. He also remarks that Faizi was 'filled with disdain' towards the Deccan sultanates of Bijapur, Ahmadnagar and Tilang Andhra because he did not recognise them as independent states, but rather as jagirs, addressing the sultans by the title of 'Mulk' such as Nizam-ul-Mulk or Qutb-ul-Mulk or simply by their names. In his book *Muhammad-Quli Qutb Shah: Founder of Haidarabad*, Sherwani says, 'His [Faizi's] solitary sentence about Muhammad Quli is "full of sneers and taunts".' This particular letter was probably written when Faizi was the imperial resident in the Deccan and is included in the collection of letters entitled variously as *Insha-i-Faizi* (Faizi's Diction), *Tabashiru's-Subh* (Early Dawn) and *Latifa-i-Faizi* (Faizi's Witticisms).

Sherwani also dismisses Faizi's reference to Bhagmati as hearsay and 'verbal jugglery' because the Mughal envoy had named an Ahmad Quli, not Muhammad Quli, and because Faizi had been based in Ahmednagar, far away from Golconda, and had never visited Hyderabad.

Other historians accuse Sherwani of pedantry, since there was no Ahmed Quli in the Qutb Shahi royal family, which means Faizi had obviously been referring to Mohammad Quli. Narendra Luther even sarcastically comments that, 'Sherwani was also writing from a distance of nearly four hundred years; spatial distance admits contemporaneity; temporal distance does not. Sherwani's own handicap is the latter.'[4]

Faizi was not Sherwani's only target. It seems as if the history professor was bound and determined to challenge and reject all references to Bhagmati made in contemporary accounts, no matter what the source.

For example, in his chronicle the *Tabaqat-i Akbar Shahi*, which he completed in about 1002 AH (1594), Nizamu'd-din Bakhshi had said: 'Muhammad Ali *(sic)* Qutbu'l-Mulk, son of Ibrahim, succeeded his father. He became so enamoured of a Hindu prostitute (patare) Bhamgasi *(sic)* by name that he founded a city which he called Bhagnagar after her and ordered that one thousand horsemen should always accompany the whore (fahisha). He has been on the throne of the kingdom for nine years now, which is 1002 years after the hijra.'[5]

This seems to leave no doubt about Bhagmati's presence in Muhammad Quli's life. But Sherwani calls Bakhshi 'a panegyric of the imperial court' and argues that since Bakhshi made 'the chronological mistake of post-dating the reign by five years to 993 instead of 988', his entire account is inaccurate.

Ferishta's chronicle, *Gulshan-i Ibrahimi*, was finished in 1609, which means his account of Golconda was written from direct living memory. According to a translation by Jonathan Scott, Ferishta had observed: 'The air of Golconda A.D. 1586 not agreeing with his constitution, he [Muhammad Quli] founded a city at about eight miles distance, which he called Bhaugnuggur, after his mistress Bhaug, a celebrated courtezan; but being afterwards ashamed of his amour, he changed it to Hyderabad, although one part of it still retains the former name of Bhagnuggur.' This again proves that Bhagmati was a real person, made of flesh and blood.

But Sherwani completely rejects Ferishta's account of his visit to Bhagnagar because of some inaccuracies such as that Muhammad Quli had been twelve years old when he ascended the throne of Golconda and that in the year 1609, the Persian ambassador Aghuzlu Sultan was still in the Deccan waiting for 'the acceptance of the proposal of marriage' of the son of Shah Abbas II with Muhammad Quli's daughter Hayat Bakshi Begum, even though the historical record showed she had already married Quli's nephew by then, the ceremonies having been conducted in the presence of the ambassador himself!

Sherwani disputes Ferishta's account since the latter had stated in his chronicle that in 1597, the Qutb Shahi army, which had been sent to help the Nizam Shahs, had fled to 'Haidarabad' after their defeat. This meant that the city could not have been called Bhagnagar in 1609 because coins had already been struck in the Hyderabad mint as early as 1603.

While rejecting references to Bhagmati, Sherwani picks sources that support his viewpoint, such as the *Tarikh-i-Muhammad Qutb Shahi*, which he calls a semi-official chronicle of the Qutb Shahi dynasty. This book describes the new city in detail but is completely silent about Bhagmati and Bhagnagar.

According to modern historian Dr Mohammed Safiullah, deputy secretary to the Government of Telengana and honorary managing trustee of the Deccan Heritage Trust, Hyderabad, Sherwani's view of Bhagmati is correct. Safiullah believes the

Muhammad Quli-Bhagmati romance is just a legend and he refuses to accept that the new city was ever called Bhagyanagar or that Bhagmati was given the title of Hyder Mahal.

'Legends add spice to history,' Safiullah tells me. 'But legends fall apart when you do a post-mortem of oral folklore.'

Safiullah says that the title 'Hyder', meaning 'lion', is a male attribute. 'It has never been given to any woman across the world. The Qutb Shahis were Shias. Hence, the city was named after Hazrat Ali, the son-in-law of Prophet Muhammad, who had the title of Hyder.'

The historian also argues that Muhammad Quli Qutb Shah mentions many women in his works, but not Bhagmati. 'Why would a sultan leave alone some of the most beautiful women in the world and fall in love with a local commoner?' he asked rhetorically.

I wanted to tell him that this is how love works! It is an emotion that doesn't consider caste, creed, religion or class. But Safiullah is unmoved.

Like other critics, Dr Safiullah, a numismatologist who claims to have the largest collection of Qutb Shahi coins in the world, also points out that there are no manuscripts, inscriptions, contemporary miniatures, coins of that period or even a grave mentioning her name.

'I have nothing against Bhagmati personally but show me one shred of evidence to prove that she existed,' Safiullah tells me. 'In fact, Allama Aijaz Farrukh had claimed that the mythical, elusive and almost alien Bhagmati was the daughter of Balan Chowdhury, the contractor of Mecca Masjid. But, his claim was without any historical or substantive basis. It was not by any empical evidence that was verifiable,' Safiullah argues. He also alludes to the fact that thirty-eight Hindu courtesans are mentioned in the Qutb Shahi records, including the better known Taramati and Pemmamati during Abdullah Qutb Shah's reign and even their graves existed in the royal necropolis. But nowhere is there any mention of Bhagmati's grave.

Safiullah's reasoning makes sense. But who is the Hyder Mahal who Muhammad Quli has himself mentioned in his verses? 'I have contacted Muslim universities across the world to know if the title Hyder Mahal was conferred upon anyone and the answers were negative. It is the fifth storey in the Khudadad Mahal, that's all,' says Safiullah.

Safiullah's vehement denial of Bhagmati's existence is countered by the beliefs of dramatist Pradeep Kumar, a retired professor of theatre at the Osmania University, who tells me that all the records concerning Bhagmati were deliberately destroyed. 'Bhagmati was from the Lingayat caste. Girls from the Lingayat caste were dedicated to the temple,' he says, which is why there is no mention of Bhagmati anywhere as per him. There might be a grain of truth in this since Bhagmati's father's name was Lingayya, according to Narendra Luther.

On the other hand, Dr P. Jogi Naidu, retired deputy director of the Department of Archaeology and Museums, Government of Telangana, insists that Bhagmati's tomb lies in Talab Katta, on the eastern side of the Charminar. In a telephone conversation with me, he says that people are not allowed to visit the tomb. 'I visited the tomb along with officials of the Tourism Department of Telengana. It was clearly visible that all inscriptions on this tomb were erased with stone. There is absolutely no doubt that the tomb is that of Bhagmati. Visitors are not permitted to enter the area.' Fascinatingly, in 1991, this unclaimed and unnamed tomb was declared to be Bhagmati's final resting place by Marri Chenna Reddy, the then chief minister of erstwhile Andhra

Pradesh, while commemorating the 400th anniversary of the city of Hyderabad.

As difficult as it already is to work out whether Bhagmati actually existed and whether or not Hyderabad was once called Bhagnagar in her honour, Abdu'l-Baqi Nihawandi has made matters more complicated in his voluminous panegyric of Abdu'r-Rahim Khan Khan-i-Khanan, the *Ma'athir-i Rahimi*, which he wrote in 1025 AH. In the book, Nihawandi has stated that Bhagnagar and Hyderabad were two completely different cities! 'Muhammad-Quli Qutb'l-mulk, son of Ibrahim Qutb'l-mulk, succeeded his father and became so much enamoured of the woman, Bhagmati, that he founded a city which he called Bhagnagar and ordered one thousand horsemen to serve her ... Towards the end of his reign he founded another city Haidarabad through the efforts of Muhammad Mu'min, one of the prominent Syeds of the city of Isfahan who held the office of Mir Jumla, and when the buildings were ready in the new capital he shifted his court thither and made it his capital.'

Although there is no direct reference to Bhagmati or Bhagnagar in the Telugu literature and chronicles of the time, some references to the city do exist in colloquial and literary forms, according to Professor Nelaturi Venkata Ramanayya who is considered a master in Vijayanagar history. In the *Rāyavācakamu*, a Telugu text composed by an anonymous writer in the court of a Madurai Nayaka after 1591, Hyderabad is referred to as Baganagaram. In fact, even the English translation of the text by Phillip B. Wagoner, titled *Tidings of the King: A Translation and Ethnohistorical Analysis of the Rāyavācakamu*, refers to Baganagaram several times. For instance: 'Addressing the problem of the text's dating, C V Ramachandra Rao ... has demonstrated unequivocally that the text must have been composed at some point between 1591—the foundation date of Baganagaram—present day—Hyderabad ...' Or for instance, 'The inclusion of Mysore, Chennapatnam [the modern Channapatna, Bangalore district], and Baganagaram [the modern Hyderabad] among the list of places to which Krishnadevaraya sends spies pushes the date of composition still later into the sixteenth century ...'

A reference to Bhagyanagaramu (as distinct from Bhagnagar or Baganagaram) occurs three times in a late sixteenth century poetical work in Telugu called *Nrishimha Vilasamu*.

Tamayya, a karnam (village official) of Golconda, had another name for the capital city. In the manuscripts *Vaijayanti Vilasamu* and *Vipranarayana Charitra*, Tamayya has called himself a resident of 'Bhagiratipattanam'. He never mentioned the name Bhagnagar in any of his works. Professor B. Rama Raju of the Telugu department of the Osmania University has said in an article titled *Sarangu Timmayya: Girvana Bhashaseva* that Tamayya was not an ordinary karnam but a peddakarnam of the capital, an officer who was like the modern mayor of a city 'who would perform the duties of a minister' and who had direct dealings with the sultan—in this case, Mohammad Quli Qutb Shah—himself.

'Bhagiratipattanam' may refer to Bhagirathi, princess of Vijayanagar who married Ibrahim Qutb Shah and was Muhammad Quli's mother. Quli mentioned his Hindu mother in his *Qulliyat*:

> *I left my faith and adopted this religion [Islam]*
> *I was born of a wonderful Hindu lady.*

Sherwani however referrs to Bhagirathi simply as 'a woman', completely ignoring her royal background as a princess of

Vijayanagar and her status in the Qutb Shahi dynasty, thus proving how prone he was to presenting important facts ambiguously to suit his arguments. But Sherwani himself makes a mistake in his book when he says that the semi-official chronicle of the Qutb Shahi dynasty, the *Tarikh-i-Muhammad Qutb Shahi*, was completed during the reign of Muhammad Qutb Shah in 1608. If the chronicle was really completed in 1608, the sultan on the throne at the time was Muhammad Quli Qutb Shah himself, not his successor, Muhammad Qutb Shah.

Sherwani's other sources of contemporary information were Mirza Nizamu'd-din Ahmad Sa'idi's Hadiqatu's *Salatin*, written in 1644, and Ali B. Taifur Bustami's *Hada'iqu's-Salatin*, written in 1681. Both books speak of the city and its founding, but neither says a word about Bhagnagar or Bhagmati. In fact, it seems Professor Sherwani was so incensed by the very concept of Bhagmati's existence that he blamed the entire Asaf Jah dynasty for the revival of the debate. In 1810, Ghulam Hussain Khan Jauhar's *Mah Nama* (History of Chanda Bai Mahalaqa), dismissed the 1782 narration by Munim Khan Hamdani of the Bhagmati legend in *Sawaneh-i-Dakan* as being completely baseless, thus bringing the love story back in focus. However, Murti explains that the *Mah Nama*'s chief source of information was the *Tarikh-i-Muhammad Qutb Shahi* which is silent on this subject, so Jauhar simply interpreted the silence as a dismissal of the legend. Sherwani too rejects *Sawaneh-i-Dakan's* mention of the legend of Bhagmati by saying: 'It is one of those publications which have simply copied down the Bhagmati legend without subjecting it to any critical analysis.'

The Bhagmati story was kept alive through that century by another Haidarabad based chronicle, *Hadiqatul Alam* (1799) written by Latif Shustari alias Abu Turab. However, Sherwani disapproves of Abu Turab's work: 'He simply places before the reader the two versions of the foundation of the new capital, one related by Ferishta, and the other by the author of *Tarikh-i-Muhammad Qutb Shahi* without any comment.' Clearly the story was uncontroversial at the time Abu Turab was writing his chronicle. It only kicked up a storm thirty-five years later, when Jauhar wrote about it in his book. In actuality, however, what was said in the chronicles of *Tarikh-i-Muhammad Qutb Shahi* and Ferishta were not incompatible. Rather, they were supplementary to each other.

Sherwani believes that the only reason for the story's appeal amongst the population of Telangana was that it was a story which was both romantic and erotic. Even where contemporary chroniclers have mentioned both Bhagmati and Bhagnagar in their work, Sherwani does his best to undermine the references. For example, while Sherwani agrees that Tavernier was probably correct in stating that the city was named Bhagnagar, he claims that the word 'Bagh' referred not to Bhagmati, but to baghs or gardens and that Tavernier was referring to a 'city of gardens'.

Sherwani, according to Murti, simply ignores Tavernier's factual mistake and without pointing it out or correcting it, he contrives to adapt the first part of the word with a slight but ingenious shift of emphasis to "Bagh" to mean garden, so that when it preceded the suffix "Nagar" which means "City", it arrived at "Bagh Nagar", meaning "City of Gardens", which fitted into his slot cogently.'

Disputes between historians aside, the matter is made more complicated by the fact that the new city was indeed a city of gardens! Historian M.A. Nayeem writes in his book *The Heritage of the Qutb Shahis of Golconda and Hyderabad* that the common people as well as the foreign travellers called the city

Bagnagar or Baghnagar simply because it had many baghs or gardens. These gardens extended from Mahal-e-Kohe Toor to Charminar to Husain Sagar and included Bagh-i-Muhammad Shahi along the eastern side of the River Musi that extended for several miles and was filled with date and coconut palms, jamun and champa trees, pomegranate, Indian almonds and grape clusters; Bagh-i-Gulshani; Bagh-i-Lingampalli; Bagh-i-Dilkush or Bagh-i-Kohe Toor; the Sultan Shahi Bagh; Phul Bagh below the Husain Sagar lake; Koh-i-Nabat Ghat, Amin Bagh; Muhammad Quli's Naddi Mahal, which had an extensive garden; a cluster of gardens surrounding the Husain Sagar over an area of four farsakhs (twelve miles); two miles of orchards and gardens belonging to the amirs that surrounded the Mahal-e-Kohe Toor (Falaknuma now); the pool-centred Gosha Mahal gardens; the gardens, groves and parks of the whole area from Naubat Ghat to Mahal-e-Kohe Toor; and the roof gardens on palaces such as the Hena Mahal.[6]

The Bagh-i-Muhammad Shahi along the eastern side of the River Musi that extended for several miles and was filled with date and coconut palms, jamun and champa trees, pomegranate, Indian almonds and grape clusters;

Thevenot mentions Bagnagar clearly. 'Heretofore the King went ever now and then to his Palace of Bagnagar, but he hath not been there this eight years; since Auran-Zeb (who was then Governour of a Province) surprized him in it, having marched his Forces with so great diligence, that they were at the Gates of Bagnagar, before the King had any News that they were marched from Aurangabad, so that he easily made himself Master of the Town: Nevertheless, the King in disguise, escaped by a private door, and retreated to the Fort of Golconda ...'

The traveller has also written about the Musi in spate: 'The river of Bagnagar beat down almost two thousand houses, in which many people perished.'

Sherwani could well have been correct in his belief that Baghnagar referred to gardens, not Bhagmati. But he has overlooked one important contemporary source who was conversant with the local language and could not possibly have confused the syllable 'ba' with 'bha'. This source was Abul Fazl.

Abul Fazl wrote in the *Akbarnama*: 'Ali Quli Khan and Muhammad Quli and Kalab Ali and Shah Beg and other dissident nobles are creating trouble in Bhagnagar.'

In fact, Jahangir, who maintained close relations with the court of Golconda, also mentions Bhagnagar in his *Tuzuk-i-Jahangiri*![7]

Certain official documents also refer to Bhagnagar. For example, the state archives contain a document of succession dated 1637 that was issued to 'Zaheeruddin, Qazi of Bhagnagar'. Historian Gijs Kruijtzer's 2008 book *Xenophobia in the Seventeenth Century India* mentions a letter that Shivaji is said to have written to Maloji Ghorpade (the Maratha ruler of the princely state of Mudhol during the British Raj and one of the former states in Southern Maratha country), which is datelined Bhagnagar. Kruijtzer says, 'The original of the letter to Maloji Ghorpade seems to have survived into the twentieth century, although no-one seems to have seen it in the past eighty-odd years. It was first taken note of in the modern period by a British officer in a Genealogy of Marratta Chiefs, published as a lithograph around 1827. The officer (possibly John Briggs) writes: "The first authentic account of this branch of the Bhonsla family [the Mudhol Ghorpades] is to be found in an original letter from Shivaji to Maloji Ghorpade, dated Bhagnuggur, when he was forming a connection with the king of Golkonda. This curious document is in the hands of Govindráv Ghorpade, together with a vast number of Persian papers, the authenticity of which, when compared with other documents of the same time, cannot, for a moment be doubted.'"

Even Pune historian Gajanan Mehendale, who is very critical of many documents originating from the Ghorpade family archives, believes that this letter, possibly about negotiations between Shivaji and the Qutb Shahis and therefore likely to be dated 1670, is 'probably authentic'.

Writing in 1884, Syed Hossain Bilgrami and C. Willmott have said that the city was 'styled Bhagnagar after one of the king's Hindu mistresses ... After her death Muhammad Quli changed the name to Haiderabad, although to the present day many natives, especially Hindus, style the city Bhagnagar.'[8]

In 1585, Mir Momin was appointed the prime minister and it was through his good offices that Muhammad Quli secured an embassy from King Abbas of Iran in 1603. But the Iranians were unlikely to be impressed by a sultan whose capital city was named after a Hindu nautch girl. According to Ziauddin Ahmed Shakeb, an expert on Indian and Islamic art, the common belief is that Mir Momin suppressed the story of Bhagmati. 'He did not appreciate the closeness between the sultan and Bhagmati. Therefore, he decided that Bhagmati's character would be driven out of contemporary history, so much so that she did not even have a tomb built over her last remains. There should be further research on Bhagmati,' he said in an article published in *The Times of India* on 22 March 2010[9]. Though Shakeb believes that there was 'a grain of truth in the character of Bhagmati and the name of Bhagnagar can be found in archival records', he also says that the sultan did not change the name of Bhagnagar to Hyderabad, nor name Hyderabad after Bhagmati.

Political developments after the conquest of Ahmadnagar by the Mughals could explain why Momin took almost a decade to start using the name Hyderabad and suppress the name associated with Bhagmati. The decade following the establishment of the new city saw Golconda involved in several political and military offensives as well as defensive operations. Since there were a number of Deccani nobles and commanders in Muhammad Quli's army and administration at the time, it is possible that Momin did not want to antagonise them by removing the name Bhagnagar altogether. But by the turn of the century, Qutb Shahi relations with Persia had peaked. In 1603, the Persian king Shah Abbas sent his envoy Prince Aghuzlu Sultan to Hyderabad, asking for the hand of the sultan's daughter Hayat Bakshi for one of his sons. Muhammad Quli received the Persian ambassador, who was accompanied by at least a hundred officials, with great pomp and extended a warm welcome along with the exchange of a large number of gifts. The Persian envoy stayed in the Qutb Shahi kingdom for six years. Since Muhammad Quli and Mir Momin were well aware of the influence and power of the Persian king and his propagation of Shia'ism, it is possible that they decided to use the name Hyderabad for official purposes because the name Bhagnagar could have been politically inconvenient. It may be no coincidence that the first coins to be struck by the Qutb Shahis after 1584 were issued from 'Darus Saltanat Hyderabad' in 1603, the year the Iranian envoy came to the kingdom.

Coinage, firmans and official missives ignored Bhagmati. Even the odes of the sultan himself did not mention Bhagmati. If at all the name Bhagnagar was used, it was used as Baghnagar—a reference to the gardens. Gardens, after all, would have been preferable to the memory of a low caste Hindu dancer named Bhagmati or Bhagyamati!

In 1656, when Aurangzeb attacked Golconda, the very last token of Bhagmati's memory was destroyed. This was a bastion known as Haideri Burj located on the southern side of Golconda fort. Had the bastion been named after Hyder, it would have been called Hyder Burj. But the name Haideri Burj seems to indicate that the bastion had been named after Bhagmati, who had been given the title of Haider Mahal by her sultan, according to Serish Nanisetti in his book *Golconda/Bagnagar/Hyderabad*. While fighting, Aurangzeb's commander Mir Miran (Asadullah Khan Bhukhari) tried to move the entrenchments closer to Haideri Burj. However Abdullah Qutb Shah's commander Musa Khan and his men blew up Mir Miran before the Mughals could take advantage of this position. The war ended three days later and a bigger bastion was built, named Musa Burj after Musa Khan, the saviour of the Golconda kingdom. The last token of Bhagmati's memory was thus removed.

Though the aristocracy sought to eliminate the name Bhagnagar (possibly after both Bhagmati and Muhammad Quli died), for the local people Bhagnagar remained the city's name. As scholar and historian Masud Husain points out in his book *Mohammad Quli Qutb Shah*, the fact that contemporary travellers such as Bernier used the name Bhagnagar showed that both names of the city were in use. Only the successors of Muhammad Quli covered up the Bhagmati episode and discouraged the further use of the name Bhagnagar, Husain adds.

There are many who, over the years, have tried to deny Bhagmati's existence, but the most damning piece of evidence against it comes from the man purported to be her lover and husband, Muhammad Quli.

Quli was a poet, a highly prolific one. He is believed to have composed about a hundred and fifty couplets a day. But nowhere in his vast repertoire of works is even a single mention of Bhagmati.

In the first manuscript of his diwan, there are fifteen poems on his twelve beloveds (Husain believes that while Quli had many more beloveds, he only wrote about his twelve favourites because there were twelve Imams). In the second manuscript, there are thirteen poems, including some dedicated to Sanwali, Kanwali, Pyari, Gori, Lala and Lalan, Mohan and Mohini, Nahni, Chabili and Mahboon. Bhagmati isn't mentioned anywhere. But in several couplets, Muhammad Quli has addressed an unnamed person he calls 'dancer'. Perhaps this was Bhagmati.

Dancer, your image is in the pupil of my heart
I prostrate myself in the arches of your eyebrows
You are my master, dancer,
Qutb Shah you have acquired a rare pearl
This dancer's art has reached perfection.[10]

One verse in particular seems to hint that the 'dancer' is Bhagmati: *She has played with her lover from her childhood days.* Quli is believed to have met Bhagmati when he was just a boy.

Three of Muhammad Quli's poems are dedicated to Haider Mahal and one to Mushtari. Mushtari is the heroine of the court poet Wajhi's romantic ballad, *Qutb Mushtari,* composed in 1609-1610. Some historians feel the name Mushtari was a veiled reference to Bhagmati, while some sources say that the sultan had asked his court poet to write a ballad based on his love affair with Bhagmati, but the name of the heroine was later changed to Mushtari. In the masnawi, Mushtari is a princess of Bengal greatly beloved by the prince, who the prince brings to the Deccan after great difficulties.

I am in love Mushtari
For your sweet lips demand
Eternal loving.

Is Mushtari Bhagmati? It's possible since Muhammad Quli wrote: *Mushtari dances for me every day*. If Mushtari was indeed a princess, isn't it unlikely that a princess would dance for the sultan every day? If Mushtari is actually Bhagmati, perhaps the fact that she is a princess in the masnawi indicates that the prejudice against her was due to her class rather than her religion. Even today, I find that Bhagmati's status as a dancer is reviled. On a recent visit to Hyderabad, when I got into a conversation about Bhagmati with a gentleman unknown to me, he said assertively: 'We would never accept a dancer as our queen.'

Bhagmati's faith could not have been a problem because Muhammad Quli wrote several couplets on his Hindu beloveds and also referred to his Hindu mother with affection and respect.

I left my faith and adopted this religion [Islam]
I was born of a wonderful Hindu lady.
I was brought up in the lap of a gracious Hindu mother.[11]

According to Ferishta, Muhammad Quli was ashamed to take Bhagmati's name, so he changed the name of the city. Since it seems unlikely that Quli was ashamed of Bhagmati's religion, it is possible that the sultanate's orthodox clergy as well as the Persian nobility who swarmed his court did not like the idea of a dancer becoming a queen.

'Muhammad Quli was too young and an immature boy on accession and was under the guardianship of very powerful senior Iranian leaders, both administrators and religious, of his father's time and they would never have allowed him to run after a prostitute and name the city after her. Unimaginable. A king need not travel five kilometres for a girl, the girl can be fetched just by slight indication. The sultan never travelled or went out alone. He was accompanied by numerous security personal staff and nobility. This is evident from the paintings,' says Nayeem in his book *The Heritage of the Qutb Shahis of Golconda and Hyderabad*.

The 'very powerful senior Iranian leaders' that Nayeem refers to controlled every aspect of the Qutb Shahi administration as well as religious matters. And the head of these leaders was prime minister Mir Momin Astrabadi, who led the governance of the kingdom. It would not be surprising therefore if the prime minister made sure that Bhagmati never became the queen or that, if Quli really did marry her, to ensure that her name did not figure anywhere in the dynasty's bloodline.

Jameela Nishat, who runs the NGO Shaheen Women Centre in the old city, suggests that I visit the area that once was Chinchlam and now is known as Shahalibanda or Bahadurpura or Mughalpura. This is where many members of the Banjara community currently live. The Banjaras are a nomadic community originally from Rajasthan and Afghanistan who centuries ago migrated to the Deccan and traded in a vast range of goods such as oilseed, sugarcane, opium, fruits and flowers, forest products and items from the hills, including tobacco and grass. Prior to the arrival of the East India Company, the Banjaras had a monopoly on the movement of salt in the Deccan plateau and the central provinces. However, in 1871, the British colonists classified them as a 'criminal tribe' and they were brought under the Criminal Tribes Act. The British then took over the trade of the goods that the Banjaras had dealt with, leaving the community impoverished and marginalised.

Jameela, who works with women in one of the areas where the Banjaras are believed to have settled, says that the Banjaras believe that Bhagmati was from their community. In fact, one of the gateways in Golconda fort is known as Banjara darwaza.

This of course is disputed. The dramatist Pradeep Kumar, a retired professor of theatre in Osmania University who did extensive research on the Banjaras as well as Bhagmati and choreographed the play *Bhagmathee*, denies that Bhagmati belonged to the community of Banjaras. 'She came, along with her family, from Karnataka and settled down in the area around Chinchlampalli,' he says.

According to Kumar, Bhagmati was a Lingayat and belonged to a family of dancers. The Lingayats dedicated their daughters to the temples, which explains why Bhagmati was considered a devadasi. Chinchlam was a village of dancers and Bhagmati often went to Nagamalleswara temple where Muhammad Quli first spotted her, Kumar adds.

Narendra Luther in his book *Hyderabad: A Biography* gives a different version of this story, writing that she was brought up by her father Lingayya since her mother died when she was eight. Meanwhile Dr Anand Raj Varma denies the possibility of Bhagmati being a Banjara and insists that she was a Telingan from the Arundhatiya community. To support his belief, Varma points out that Muhammad Quli's own verses include words such as '*chhori*' and 'Telingan'.

Nevertheless, Jameela thinks I should meet some of the Banjaras to find out if they consider Bhagmati one of their own, so she assigns three young women to guide me in my quest to establish the existence of Bhagmati—Pooja, Zaira and Archana.

Most Banjaras now work as construction labourers. But many of them were at home the day I set off to meet them. Pooja, Zaira and Archana take me from house to house so that I can ask them about Bhagmati. Yes, they all say, they have heard of the dancer queen. But they have no idea if she had been one of them.

Our last stop is a cemetery called Meer ka Daira. Though I know Bhagmati has no grave to her name, I decide to take a tour around the place because this area had earlier been a Brahmin settlement and part of Chinchlam, Bhagmati's village. Shah Chirag, a sufi saint, was the first Muslim to inhabit this place and according to his wishes, as mentioned earlier, he was buried here. Several years later, Mir Momin Astrabadi purchased this land, mixed the holy earth of Karbala with its soil and donated it to the people for the free burial of the dead. His own resting place is in this cemetery. What can be more ironic than the fact that the man who denied Bhagmati a grave now lies buried in her village?

Our guide points me towards Mir Momin Astrabadi and Shah Chirag's graves. I ask about Bhagmati. Where is her grave? The authorities at the cemetery have no idea. I have reached a literal dead end.

Back at home, I decide to stop looking for physical symbols of Bhagmati's existence but seek her instead in literature and the arts. Men of power may have deleted her name from the royal hagiography, but her popularity among the people has not diminished for centuries.

In her paper *Courtesans of Hyderabad and Beyond: Claiming Significance,* historian and anthropologist Karen Leonard mentions the names of three legendary courtesans—Bhagmati, Taramati and Pemmamati. Leonard uses the term 'popular belief' in her references to Bhagmati's legend, the founding of the city of Bhagyanagar and on the dancer becoming queen after being titled Hyder Mahal. There is definite proof of the existence of the two other courtesans and in fact, a caravan sarai built by Taramati exists even today and is used for cultural performances.

Leonard's paper sets me thinking that had Muhammad Quli not married Bhagmati and made her his queen, she might have had a tomb perhaps or at least some sort of memorial to mark her final resting place. But in marrying her, Quli inadvertently relegated her to the realms of imagination.

Nevertheless, Bhagmati has never been forgotten by the people of her land. Even today, they continue to honour her memory through different forms of art and folk traditions.

In 1991, the legendary Kuchipudi danseuse Swapna Sundari produced a dance drama based on the Muhammad Quli-Bhagmati love story in which she portrayed the role of Bhagmati and dance guru Shri Kalakrishna performed as the young sultan. On a recent visit to Hyderabad, I met Professor Kalakrishna at the Potti Shri Ramulu Telugu university and asked him about Bhagmati. Kalakrishna insisted that Bhagmati was indeed a devadasi who performed at the Nagamalleswara temple. In those days, devadasis trained for seven or eight years and then dedicated their lives to the temple deity. Kalakrishna also believes that Bhagmati perhaps travelled with her mother as a part of the entourage of Queen Bhagirathi from Vijayanagar to the kingdom of Golconda and took up lodgings in the Hindu part of the kingdom of Golconda, namely Chinchlam. Hence, the confusion that she was one of the Banjaras.

The dance drama performed by Swapna Sundari and Shri Kalakrishna is just one of many activities and events built around the love story of Bhagmati and Muhammad Quli. In 2020, in the third edition of Shehr-e-Ishq, a series of historical walking tours of Hyderabad organised by Hyderabad Trails, participants toured the Qutb Shahi tombs and heard the story of Bhagmati during an event called *Quli—the Prince of Hearts*.

In January 2011, a literary dance drama called *Bhagyanagaram* was staged at Ravindra Bharati. Its subject was the well-known love story of Bhagmati and Muhammad Quli.

Sometime in the 1980s, filmmaker Muzaffar Ali made a short movie on Muhammad Quli Qutb Shah and Bhagmati. In the film, Hayat Bakshi is portrayed as the daughter of Muhammad Quli and his first wife. We now know that it is unlikely that Muhammad Quli's first wife could have been Hayat Bakshi's mother because she left the city soon after the Naldurg battle in the early 1580s, while Hayat was born in 1592. (Sherwani too categorically asserts that Hayat Bakshi was the daughter of Muhammad Quli's first wife.)

Muzaffar Ali's film showed several events such as Muhammad Quli naming the new city Bhagnagar, Bhagmati marrying the sultan, Bhagmati being conferred with the title of Haider Mahal and Muhammad Quli renaming the city Hyderabad thereafter.

The Qutb Shahi kingdom of Golconda followed a strange practice first noted in 1614, which finds mention in a book of essays called *Relations of Golconda in the Early Seventeenth Century*, edited by W.H. Moreland. According to one of the writers, 'Every year, in the month of April, the prostitutes of the whole kingdom travelled to Bagnagar, whither they were summoned by a

"Maldaer" (a sort of tipstaff), to dance in celebration of the death of the first Muslim King.' Both Ferishta[12] and Faizi have referred to Bhagmati as a courtesan. This may explain why the courtesans gathered in Bhagnagar every year. Though no one can say which community she belonged to, one thing is certain. Bhagmati lived in Chinchlam, the place where the Charminar stands today.

According to popular belief, Haider Mahal was the title that Muhammad Quli bestowed upon Bhagmati after making her his wife and queen. One of his verses clearly indicated his intention to make Haider Mahal the queen.

Give thanks to the prophet that you found this woman
Haider deserves to wear a crown.

Clearly, Haider Mahal was special to Quli and her social status was higher than Quli's other beloveds. Since Haider Mahal is also the name of the third storey of the Khudadad Mahal, Quli wrote: *Sing only the charm of Haider in Haider Mahal.* A smart monarch he was indeed!

Quli wrote three poems on Haider Mahal, such as the one below:

Haider Mahal is as sweet as sugar
Day after day is full of enjoyment and love
Her tall stature sparkles like the navratan
All the lovely maidens are nothing before her
She wears the jewel of love on her forehead
Which shines and twinkles like the navratan
Wearing the shawl of love, she looks
Like the red velvet beetle
Her antics put to shame even the best coquettes.

Professor Husain believes that the dancer Quli mentions in several couplets is a reference to the dancer from Chinchlam.

Walking and sleeping I see only you
Wherever I look, everywhere is the dancer.[13]

In another poem, Quli has mentioned a Haider Pyari.

Bhagmati was also a popular muse for artists, with several paintings depicting her as a queen. According to P. Jogi Naidu, from 1750 onwards, the Deccan School of Art represented Bhagmati in miniatures and paintings. The mirth and luxury prevalent during Qutb Shahi rule, which was especially enhanced during the reign of Muhammad Quli, have also been effectively portrayed in the miniature paintings of the Golconda and Hyderabad Schools of art.

For instance, one miniature painting from the period depicts a king and queen seated on a throne with cups in their hands, watching a dance performance as musicians play. The faces of the women in this painting, including that of the queen, appear to be Deccani in nature. The verse at the top of the painting says: 'God has given to Qutb Shah a lovely lady to be loved due to his prayer and his being the slave ardent worshipper of God.' Muhammad Quli's first wife was Persian and there is no mention of any other queen in the Qutb Shahi historical records. Is this the lovely lady Bhagmati?

B. Lavanya, in her paper on royal and ordinary women in Golconda miniature paintings titled *Representation of Women in the Miniature Paintings in the Deccan School,* observes that the women seem to be painted by a Bukhara artist because the colours are thick and match the Bukhara sensibility. However, the women are dressed in the Golconda style. The king, who is seated on the throne with the queen in some pictures, is

Muhammad Quli Qutb Shah as indicated by the scribe and the painter. Several influences are seen in these miniatures, signifying that Golconda was a cosmopolitan place with diverse influences and that Deccani artists worked side by side with other artists. However, despite Persian and European influences such as the depiction of angels, Deccani features are discernible, mainly in the use of mineral colours like the bluish-purple and salmon-red that are typical of the Golconda School of painting.

'The queen depicted in some paintings enthroned with the king is none other than the mistress of Muhammad Quli Qutb Shah, the beautiful Hindu dancer Bhagmati. She is depicted dressed in a mixture of Hindu and Muslim fashion, with a long designful *(sic)* skirt and dupatta over her head which covers her body. She is shown wearing slippers, a rare feature of Deccani painting,' writes Lavanya.

A similar painting depicts a woman believed to be Bhagmati standing beneath a tree with another woman. Bhagmati wears a transparent skirt and seems to be enjoying the natural beauty surrounding her as well as the wine offered by the other woman. The costumes of the queen and her companions are all richly decorated, indicating that the luxury and status enjoyed by ordinary women at Deccani courts was equal to that of royal women. Romance was a popular theme in Golconda miniature paintings, which depicted the lives of different women in the framework of medieval Deccan royalty and society and presented a kaleidoscope of their lives in the Qutb Shahi kingdom.

An eighteenth century painting of Bhagmati displayed in the government museum depicts her as a lady of high status. According to Nayeem, the lady in the painting could be anyone, but the museum believes it is Bhagmati depicted as a queen.

'The paintings made during the eighteenth and nineteenth centuries that depict the prostitute are just imaginative, aiming to tell a fictitious story,' notes Nayeem.

So even the arts give us no real answers to the question of Bhagmati's existence. Yet books will still be written with Bhagmati as their muse, movies will still be made, poems will still be composed and recited and prayers will still be offered in temples and mosques in her name. Bhagmati will live on for at least another few centuries, her story repeated again and again, her presence nearly tangible in the streets of Hyderabad and its bazaars, in the city's majestic monuments, in the rivers and gardens, in the mosques and temples, but above all in the hearts of the people of Hyderabad.

Dagh Dehlvi, who was buried in the same cemetery as Mir Momin Astrabadi and the twentieth century maestro Bade Ghulam Ali Khan, has acknowledged the love story behind the construction of Hyderabad in a couplet:

Hazāroñ kaam mohabbat meñ haiñ maze ke 'dagh' …
Jo log kuchh nahíñ karte kamāl karte haiñ.

(There are thousands of pleasurable tasks to be performed in love, Dagh …
Those who don't do anything [love], do nothing.)

If Bhagmati hadn't existed, would Hyderabad have been built? The answer is probably yes. But the city might not have been as grand as it turned out to be. Muhammad Quli's vision was driven by the power of love. And love, as we all know, survives forever.

CHAPTER 5

Hyderabad – An Ode to Love

It is a resort of heavenly peace and worldly comfort, it gives solace to the human heart and comfort to the human body; its population is even larger than the human mind can think of; its buildings are loftier than human intellect can imagine; its air is so refreshing and the flow of fountains so sweet, and its verdures so pleasant and invigorating that the flowers and the vegetation of this land may be compared with the glitter and colour of emerald and ruby.[1]

—Mohammad Saqi, Aurangzeb's court chancellor who was present during the siege of Golconda, writing about the city of Hyderabad

After raiding the Golconda fort, Aurangzeb toured the kingdom's new capital of Bhagnagar, built less than a hundred years earlier. He was escorted by Nemat Ali Khan, a Qutb Shahi noble. As they rode past a palace, the Mughal emperor pulled up his horse, exclaiming that it was a very tall building. Clearly, he had never seen a building of such height before, which confirmed the testimony of foreign visitors that Bhagnagar was bigger and better built than the Mughal capitals of Lahore and Agra.[2]

The palace that Aurangzeb saw was the Dad Mahal or the palace of justice. 'Rather say Shaddad Mahal,' Aurangzeb is believed to have said sarcastically, Shaddad being a king he had just defeated.

The Qutb Shahi noble replied calmly, 'Sire, only those who are high minded can build high rise buildings.' Apparently Aurangzeb was so taken aback at this retort that he cut short his tour of the city and appointed his son Prince Azam as its governor.

After ruling for some time, Azam wrote to his father, asking for an increase in his allowance. When Aurangzeb told him to shift to one of the Qutb Shahi palaces, the prince apparently replied that he wouldn't be able to afford even the lighting expenses of the palace!

Such was the glorious Qutb Shahi kingdom which was razed to dust by the Mughals. But even though it has been destroyed, neither the new rulers nor the sands of time have been able to erase the footprints left behind by a civilisation that changed the equation between the two religious communities of Hindus and Muslims forever.

Most people refer to Hyderabad's Ganga-Jamuni tehzeeb or culture as 'syncretic'. By this, they mean the melding of different faiths, such as Hinduism and Islam. But the word 'syncretic' doesn't really apply to Hyderabad, says historian and anthropologist Karen Leonard. While Hyderabadi culture is syncretic, Hyderabadi society is not.

'I do not take these Indo-Muslim practices as evidence of a cultural synthesis or syncretism or hybridity,' Leonard writes. 'Rather, they are evidence of a successful plural society with an elite or ruling culture that powerfully shaped the lives of people throughout the city.'[3]

Hyderabad, though ruled by Muslims continuously, was never declared an Islamic state. Though all its rulers modelled the court culture on the Persian court, neither the Qutb Shahis nor the Nizams (except the last Nizam after Partition) ever tried to impose Islamic law or convert their subjects to Islam. Thus, a common cultural thread was created which bound the two main communities with each other while allowing them to maintain their separate faiths in their own way. The nature of this thread can be seen in the old city, which has two distinctly different neighbourhoods adjacent to one another, one Muslim, the other Hindu. Members of both communities co-exist peacefully and mingle freely as neighbours and have done so for generations. It is telling that the only recorded instances of communal clashes are dated to the twentieth and twenty-first centuries. In Leonard's view, the culture of the city of Hyderabad is Indo-Muslim in nature. 'Muslim rather than Islamic emphasises a civilisational and not a religious culure ... Not only the court and administrative culture but the urban culture as well was Indo-Muslim or Mughlai, at the neighbourhood and even the household level. All who lived in the city, especially in the neighbourhoods of the old walled city, participated in that dominant public culture, regardless of their religious affiliations and private religious observances,' she writes.

I lived in Hyderabad for more than four years. This was when Chandrababu Naidu, the son-in-law of the actor turned politician N.T. Rama Rao, was the chief minister of undivided Andhra Pradesh. Over the next ten years, the laidback, self-indulgent and languid city transformed into an ultra-modern metro. The driving force behind this transformation was the Information Technology (IT) sector. The swanky new cluster of IT outfits became known as Cyberabad, the latest attraction for tourists and professionals alike.

But neither modernisation nor the emergence of Cyberabad changed the character of Hyderabad. Hyderabad, in fact, with its hybrid culture and vast range of cultural influences, has turned the diverse population of the city into a cohesive, unified whole. Despite the demands of the ever-changing world, the people of Hyderabad hold on to their past with a fierce determination because this past is shared between all the communities of the city. In this common past of cultural diversity lies Hyderabad's homogeneity, its tehzeeb, its character.

For example, the potentially explosive topic of Shia-Sunni differences is carefully avoided in Hyderabad. When I questioned a revered Allama in the old city about clashes between the Shia and Sunni sects, he quite sternly told me not to ever bring up the topic again, since it was unheard of in Hyderabad. There is solidarity between the different sects of the Muslim population, solidarity between locals and immigrants, solidarity between Hindus and Muslims, solidarity between the upper classes and the lower classes and solidarity between different linguistic and professional groups. Both the ruling elite and the local elite of the city have always spoken a variety of languages—Marathi, Telugu, Kannada, Persian, Urdu, Dakhni and Hindi. Muslims have been the majority of the urban, ruling elite while Hindus have formed the bulk of rural peasantry.[4] Hindus have also held some powerful administrative appointments. Hyderabad is no one community's fiefdom. The city belongs to its people—*all* its people. They keep the flame of brotherhood simmering. A common cultural identity comprises the character of the city. Hyderabad is not any particular community's religious or linguistic inheritance.

Political parties frequently try to spark communalism in this great city, but the people of Hyderabad stubbornly ignore it, preferring to identify themselves as 'Hyderabadi' rather than as

Hindu or Muslim. But as India becomes ever more polarised in terms of religion, Hyderabadis have begun clinging to the past even more in a desperate attempt to preserve their cultural legacy.

Through the centuries, the ethnic Telugu-speaking people of the region have intermingled and amalgamated with the people who migrated to Golconda. Craftsmen and traders who came between the sixteenth and the nineteenth centuries were invited by the rulers to build and embellish the forts, tombs and other structures. This mingling between those of different regions and lands led to the emergence of Urdu, with its colourful locally spoken version known as Hyderabadi Urdu or Dakhniboli.

The Qutb Shahi rulers adopted liberal economic policies and patronised literary works irrespective of the religion, caste and language of the creators. Administration, literature, education, art, architecture, dance, music and daily life all grew into shining examples of Golconda's composite culture. Social functions such as the marriage of Hazrat Qasim (the son of Imam Hasan and nephew of Imam Hussain) and stories of Muharram and Imam Hussain were popular themes of Telugu literature. Many Hindu marriage and festival customs were adopted by Muslims. Hindu Gods such as Ram and Krishna provided themes for literary works dedicated by the Hindus to the Qutb Shahi sultans. Kirtans or gatherings for devotional singing were freely held and temples were constructed without interference.[5] Muhammad Quli wrote of himself:

Hindu reetku tum dete hain riwaja
Kebut khananam ne hain toh bhi hamansar.
(You give encouragement to Hindu practices—that is the accusation. After all the temple is also like the mosque.)[6]

According to Narendra Luther, Muhammad Quli's poetry substantiates the general view about his complete identification with his people. Hindu religious activities were encouraged all over Andhra Desa and the villagers of the Telugu speaking Deccan region made traditional Muslim stories part of their literature and culture. As a gesture of good will, the Qutb Shahi rulers made Telugu as well as Persian a language of administration. Many Hindus were part of aristocratic groups and held high administrative positions.[7]

It was during the Qutb Shahi period that Hyderabad became the centre for the development of Dakhni Urdu. In fact, Muhammad Quli contributed to the development of Dakhni Urdu the most. The language was mixed, derived from Persian, Arabic, Sanskrit, Telugu, Marathi and Hindi. The style of the language was simple, penetrating and appealing. Persian ghazals were translated into Dakhni poetry. Original poems were composed in Dakhni Urdu. Prose writing also developed and both secular and religious stories were written. Persian and Telugu edicts were issued. Towards the end of the Qutb Shahi dynasty, these were primarily in Telugu with summaries in Persian. According to Indologist Richard Eaton, as the sultans adopted Telugu, they saw their territory as Telugu-speaking and their polity as a Telugu-speaking state, with the elites of the sultanate viewing their rulers as Telugu Sultans.[8] In 1634, during the reign of Abdullah Qutb Shah, *Ratirahasya*, a medieval Sanskrit text on love and sex by Pandit Kokkoka, was translated into Persian and titled *Lazzat-un-Nisa* (*Flavours of the Woman*).

But those who have been born and brought up in Hyderabad and have seen the city evolve over the past three or four decades tend to agree that some element of the Hyderabadi tehzeeb is now missing. Exactly what this missing element might be is difficult to identify. But the creeping sense of fear and apprehension slowly crawling through the ethos of the city seems to indicate that the social and secular tolerance that defined Hyderabadi tehzeeb has been diluted; that even though many Hyderabadis still retain a secular spirit, by now the fact that it is a part of their tradition seems to be more myth and memory than the present truth. Politicians are responsible for this change in the city's character, but many Hyderabadis are still holding on to their cultural roots, still fighting divisive politics, still trying to preserve the last remnants of a civilisation that carved for itself a unique place in India's social and cultural fabric.

Hyderabad's Ganga-Jumna tehzeeb has been nurtured and practised by its residents for more than three hundred and fifty years. Its origin lies in the rule of the Qutb Shah dynasty, especially in the love story of Muhammad Quli and Bhagmati. Whether or not Bhagmati existed, no matter who took the throne and who was ousted from it, the love story remains alive. I will wager that it will never die. It *should* never die.

Hyderabad was ruled uninterruptedly by Muslim kings from its foundation to its incorporation into the Republic of India. It has had a reputation for communal harmony for most of its pre-Independence existence. The people of the city will never want to forget the love story that lies at the very core of the city, for in it lies the genesis of the peace and brotherhood between the two major communities of the Indian subcontinent. It is true that Muhammad Quli was not the first king in his family to marry a Hindu woman. His mother Bhagirathi was a Hindu princess from Vijayanagar. But Bhagmati was not only a Hindu, but also Muhammad Quli's only wife after the departure of his first wife. No historical record mentions any other wife or royal consort. No grave memorialises any other queen or wife of Muhammad Quli. So Bhagmati's name is remembered even today.

Could Bhagmati have influenced Muhammad Quli's way of life and governance? Perhaps. More likely however is the fact that Quli and his father Ibrahim before him were supported by Hindu naikwaris and certain Hindu nobles, such as Raya Rao, so having a Hindu queen was not considered unusual.

However, this brings me back to my original question. Was the city of Hyderabad constructed as a grand gesture of Muhammad Quli's love for Bhagmati or was it the product of practicality?

The answer is not an easy one.

Muhammad Quli wasn't the first Qutb Shahi sultan to think of moving out of Golconda fort. Given the congestion in the fort, his father Ibrahim had been thinking of doing the same thing. But when Ibrahim died, the task became Muhammad Quli's responsibility. By the time Quli took the throne, the population of the Golconda fort had exploded. Apart from the nobles and retainers, there were more than forty thousand military men. The shortage of water and the fort's open drains led to insanitary conditions and resulted in epidemics such as the plague and cholera. According to Abdul Qadeer Khan Bidri in *Ahwal-i-Tarikh-i-Farkhunda*, the nobility of Golconda submitted a petition to Muhammad Quli for an alternative place. Urged by his subjects, Muhammad Quli decided to build a new city.

Now, even though the original idea to build this new city might not have been Quli's, the location the new sultan settled upon was probably influenced by his love affair with Bhagmati.

Even then it seems far-fetched that Quli built a whole city for Bhagmati. He might have been in love, but he was not foolish. He had a kingdom to take care of and the welfare of his subjects to keep in mind. So the construction of the city was as much a matter of governance as it might have been of love.

In his paper *The Hunt for a Location: Narratives on the Foundation of Cities in South and Southeast Asia*, architect and cultural historian Pushkar Sohoni explains the role of 'foundation stories' in the historical narratives of cities. While historical documents are important, so are the stories told by the people of the cities themselves about how and why their cities came to be founded where they were. These stories need not be contemporary. They could just as well have been written in a later period or passed down through generations orally.

Sherwani believes that the location was chosen by Quli pragmatically and since Chinchlam was located on the busy road to Masulipatnam, it encouraged mercantile traffic. On the other hand, one of the foundation stories of Hyderabad speaks of the presence of a Bhagyalakshmi temple in Chinchlam, which apparently gave Bhagmati her name and her profession of devadasi or dancer. This foundation story also says that the spot where Bhagmati and Muhammad Quli first met became the centre point of the new city, which came up around it.

But there is yet another foundation story, this one based on heirophany or divine intervention. This is the story of the tazia that was set up at a spot already designated as the centre of the new city when the plague hit Golconda.

In this story, the city centre lay at the crossroads of two national caravan routes and following the plague, Muhammad Quli knelt down at the spot and prayed. 'Take pity on my poor subjects and deliver us from the pestilence, Allah,' he begged. 'And I shall erect a magnificent monument on this very site, so all people may remember and respect forever your wondrous powers and inestimable kindness.'[9]

Within days the plague ended and people started to recover miraculously. True to his word, Quli built the monument he had promised and this was the Charminar around which developed the city of Hyderabad.

According to Sohoni, the foundation story of a city sends a powerful message, 'one that performed a number of functions, including the mediation of several traditions.' As explained by classical archaeologist Naoíse Mac Sweeney, post-modernist theories and literary criticism have allowed foundation myths to be read as social constructs rather than merely as documentary history. Accordingly, these 'myths are not dispassionate documentary chronicles ... instead they are complicated literary creations, their form and content carefully tailored in accordance with certain agenda and expectations.'[10]

Thus in choosing this site, Muhammad Quli served two purposes. One, that his beloved wouldn't have to travel all the way from Chinchlam to Golconda, and two, that the capital would be strategically located in terms of trade and business. The fact that the new city was aesthetically perfect reflected Muhammad Quli's own penchant for all things beautiful. So while a new city would have been built anyway, Quli's love for Bhagmati might have served as a catalyst.

Muhammad Quli died early at the age of forty-six, but his rule was fairly peaceful and productive. He lived a contented life as much by providence as by his own efforts. He wanted a new capital, he built one. He wanted to be close to his paramour, so he chose a site that would facilitate his meetings with her and also benefit his kingdom. He allowed his Persian prime minister to design and build the city as per his wishes, he kept his clergy happy by building the Charminar, which adhered to the tenets of his religion's architecture. He built a mosque and ashurkhana and established a madarsa for students. And of course, he kept his royal family and his subjects equally happy by building palaces, bazaars, mohallas.

He had everything a monarch could ask for except for one

thing—a queen, without whom he could not have an heir. He brought home Bhagmati and to appease different factions, gave her the new name of Hyder Mahal, which was based on the name of the prophet's son-in-law Hyder. Evidently, Muhammad Quli ensured that Bhagmati was very much a part of the new city, although he changed the name of the city from Bhagnagar to Hyderabad even before his queen had died.

There were political reasons for the change of name. Though by their patronage of arts and force of arms the Qutb Shahis had secured authority over the Telugus, new problems had emerged in the north. The Mughals had captured Ahmednagar and its queen Chand Bibi was dead. Malik Ambar was defeated in 1601. In order to face the growing threat of the Mughals, Muhammad Quli needed the support of the more orthodox Muslims. So Quli minted the first coins from Hyderabad in 1603 while Bhagmati was still alive and used the name Hyderabad for all official correspondence.

At the same time, there was no official denial of the name Bhagnagar, partly because an official denial would have alienated the affections of the indigenous people, especially his Hindu subjects, and partly because the sultan may have wanted to remain faithful to the memory of his first love. So the name Bhagnagar continued to be in use until the end of the seventeenth century, along with the name Hyderabad.

Some politicians today however reject the name Bhagnagar. Instead, they claim the city was originally called Bhagyanagar—even though no contemporary chronicler has ever recorded this name. Their argument is based on a Bhagyalakshmi temple that is adjacent to the Charminar.

But, according to old residents of the city, this temple was first simply a place where an old woman worshipped a small stone and asked for alms. Then, in the 1960s, it became a small shrine, and finally, in the 1990s, it became a pucca structure with an idol. In 2012, addressing a RTI query sent by heritage activist, S.Q. Maqsood, the Archaeological Survey of India (ASI) replied in no uncertain terms that the temple dedicated to goddess Lakshmi was an unauthorised construction.

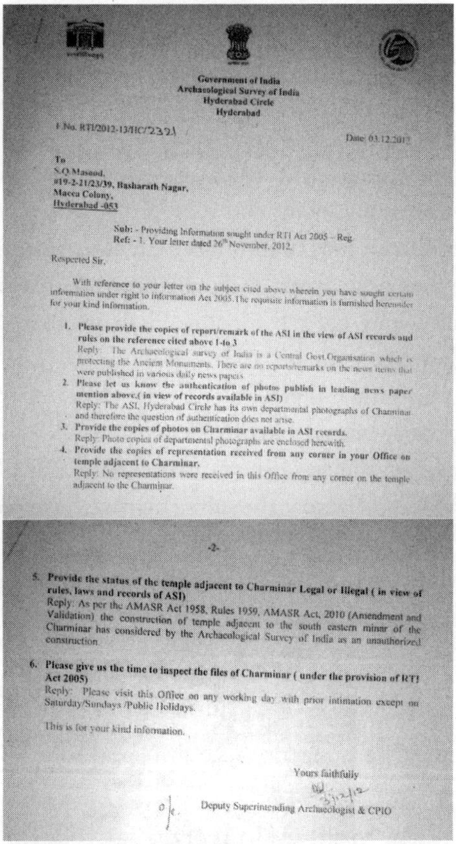

Government of India
Archaeological Survey of India
Hyderabad Circle
Hyderabad

F.No. RTI/2012-13/HC/2321

Date: 03.12.2012

To
S.Q.Masood,
#19-2-21/23/39, Basharath Nagar,
Macca Colony,
Hyderabad -053

Sub: - Providing Information sought under RTI Act 2005 – Reg.
Ref: - 1. Your letter dated 26th November, 2012.

Respected Sir,

With reference to your letter on the subject cited above wherein you have sought certain information under right to information Act 2005. The requisite information is furnished hereunder for your kind information.

1. **Please provide the copies of report/remark of the ASI in the view of ASI records and rules on the reference cited above 1-to 3**
   Reply: The Archaeological survey of India is a Central Govt.Organisation which is protecting the Ancient Monuments. There are no reports/remarks on the news items that were published in various daily news papers.
2. **Please let us know the authentication of photos publish in leading news paper mention above.(in view of records available in ASI)**
   Reply: The ASI, Hyderabad Circle has its own departmental photographs of Charminar and therefore the question of authentication does not arise.
3. **Provide the copies of photos on Charminar available in ASI records.**
   Reply: Photo copies of departmental photographs are enclosed herewith.
4. **Provide the copies of representation received from any corner in your Office on temple adjacent to Charminar.**
   Reply: No representations were received in this Office from any corner on the temple adjacent to the Charminar.

-2-

5. **Provide the status of the temple adjacent to Charminar Legal or Illegal (in view of rules, laws and records of ASI)**
   Reply: As per the AMASR Act 1958, Rules 1959, AMASR Act, 2010 (Amendment and Validation) the construction of temple adjacent to the south eastern minar of the Charminar has considered by the Archaeological Survey of India as an unauthorized construction.
6. **Please give us the time to inspect the files of Charminar (under the provision of RTI Act 2005)**
   Reply: Please visit this Office on any working day with prior intimation except on Saturday/Sundays /Public Holidays.

This is for your kind information.

Yours faithfully

Deputy Superintending Archaeologist & CPIO

ASI letter (Photo courtesy: Dr Mohammed Safiullah)

However, the builders of this temple claim that it has existed for centuries and that the Charminar was constructed near it. This is simply not true: when this issue became controversial once again in 2012, several magazines and newspapers published old photographs which showed that the presence of the temple was only from 1990s onwards. As further proof, Serish Nanisetti, in his book *Golconda/Bagnagar/Hyderabad,* has published a 1915 map by Leonard Munn, an engineer recruited by the Nizam of Hyderabad to map the city, that clearly shows there was no Bhagyalakshmi temple in the southeast corner of Charminar. According to Nanisetti, the temple came up only forty years ago. Making this an election issue now is not justified. It simply creates unnecessary conflict.

Hyderabad-based playwright Mohammad Ali Baig, whose famous play *Dilon-ka-Shehzaada* revolves around the love story of Quli Qutub Shah and Bhagmati, says that none of this should matter today. 'Whether Bhagmati existed or not has no bearing on the name of a city. The controversy is only a part of a clear political agenda. It doesn't change the history of a city,' he says.

It is true however that Bhagnagar existed.

In June 2022, Hyderabad city's Right to Information activist Robin Zacheus asked the ASI for historic evidence of the use of the names Bhagnagar and/or Bhagyanagar such as coins, inscriptions or miniatures from the period. He also asked why and when the city was renamed Hyderabad and whether the ASI had any record of a proposal by Sardar Patel to change Hyderabad's name. It is said that Sardar Patel, to counter the Nizam's decision to declare Hyderabad an Islamic state, coined the term 'Ek Bharat' (Akhand Bharat). This was what the Prime Minister of India Narendra Modi said during the executive meet of his party, the Bharatiya Janata Party (BJP), in Hyderabad in 2022. Since then, BJP stalwarts have picked up the point to impel a change of name for Hyderabad.

Zacheus also asked the ASI for any record or evidence of the Bhagyalakshmi temple having existed where the Charminar stands today. In its reply, the ASI Hyderabad circle stated, 'None of the monuments/sites under the jurisdiction of Archaeological Survey of India, Hyderabad circle in the Telangana state, has any evidence of ancient mosques built on Hindu religious sites.'

In 1979, the temple, then still a shrine, became a target when an armed group seized the grand mosque in Mecca and the Majlis-E-Ittehadul Muslimeen (MIM; now known as the All India Majlis-E-Ittehadul Muslimeen) called for a bandh in the old city. When the Hindu shopkeepers of the area requested the MIM to allow them to keep their shops open as it was Diwali, there were clashes. Four years later, the temple became the site of communal clashes once again after saffron organisations put up big cloth banners in the area and called for the declaration of India as a Hindu republic. When a Muslim man threw a stone at the temple, the saffron organisations desecrated a mosque in retaliation, prompting Muslim leaders to call for a bandh. This resulted in clashes that killed forty-five people.

Now the Bhagyalaksmi temple is back in focus due to the political patronage it has received from the BJP. Many people find this disturbing. Dr Safiullah says that 'though the Charminar is a listed heritage monument in the "A" category of monuments, it was denied a World Heritage tag because of the illegal and unauthorised structure at the southeastern corner, a fact that was brought to the notice of the then Government of Andhra Pradesh by the International Council on Monuments and Sites and World Monuments Fund team which came to survey the monument in 2013 and 2018.'

This is a divisive game that the two sides can play endlessly while people suffer and the city's heritage corrodes. While one group of politicians wants to change the name of Hyderabad to Bhagyanagar after Bhagyamati, the dancer who married a Muslim king for love, another group claiming the same faith as Muhammad Quli Qutb Shah denies the existence of Bhagmati altogether. It is important to know that the lady was not called Bhagyamati but Bhagmati (as per contemporary records) and deliberately distorting her name or denying her existence altogether will serve no purpose other than creating unnecessary communal tension, and more importantly, causing irremediable damage to our heritage.

All the different aspects of Hyderabadi tehzeeb grew on the soil of romanticism. 'Images of charm and romance, grandeur and splendour [were] woven with legend, which over the years continued to inspire contemporary folklore.'[11] I sometimes wonder: if this love story had not been narrated over and over across four centuries, would Hyderabadis still have the passion to preserve their Ganga-Jumna tehzeeb?

In her paper *Changing Facets of Hyderabadi Tehzeeb: Are We Missing Anything?*, Dr Vinita Pandey, professor of Sociology at Nizam College, Osmania University, quotes Narendra Luther on the difference between two emblems of love: the Taj Mahal in Agra and the city of Hyderabad. The Taj Mahal, Luther says, symbolised a 'pining for a departed beloved soul, Bhagyanagar was a celebration of a union of lovers. Taj was to enshrine a resting place for a departed queen, Bhagyanagar to provide living space for her subjects.'

I have lived in Hyderabad for a long time and for me, the city was, the city is, and the city will forever be an ode to love—the love that its king, Sultan Mohammad Quli Qutb Shah, shared with his queen Bhagmati. This love is cherished, nurtured and kept alive in the hearts of Hyderabad's people and in the city's lanes and bazaars even today. Mohammad Quli's old Hyderabad lures tourists and pilgrims alike with a unique flavour synonymous with love. This love survived the Mughals, the Nizams, and even the communal clashes of post-Independence India. Bhagmati not only brought joy to her lover Muhammad Quli's life, but she gave the people of Hyderabad a reason to celebrate love. The people of Hyderabad cling to their past not because they want to remain trapped in a time warp but because the romance of the sultan and the dancer has given them a unique identity and the hope that not all love stories end tragically.

Usne kitni tabahiyan dekhi
Uske zakhmo ka kuch hisab nahin
Bawajood iske is zamaane mein
Mere Hyderabad ka jawab nahin.

—'Kamal' Prasad Kamal[12]

Acknowledgements

For me, Hyderabad has always been a warm and welcoming city. Never for a moment did I feel like an outsider there, nor did I ever feel isolated. In fact, I would say I was just not allowed to be alone. Wherever I went and whoever I met, I was greeted with open arms. There was an infectious energy to the city that never failed to charge up the atmosphere. The city's exuberance matched my excitement at starting a new life there. Over the years that I lived in the city, I made many friends to last me a lifetime, some of whom were by my side all along while I wrote this book.

It was Dr Vijay Kumar Tadakamalla who put me on the trail of this story. I can say without hesitation that if it hadn't been for him, I would have been clueless about how to proceed. I extend my heartfelt thanks to him for his constant support, and for putting me in touch with some of the city's top academics and intellectuals who became the guiding forces behind the book. The first among them was late Dr Anand Raj Varma, who despite his advanced age took us around the city and connected me to some of the most revered academics in the field. His books have been a major source of information for me. Unfortunately, Dr Varma passed away within a few months of our meeting, but I remain indebted to him for his valuable assistance and encouragement.

One of the most stimulating exchanges that took place during the course of my research was at the office of the well-known historian and intellectual, Dr Sajjad Shahid, where we had a rather interesting session with him, Dr Varma and popular journalist and social activist, Mr Mir Ayoob Ali Khan. I feel privileged to have been a part of such an engaging discussion that provided me with both relevant information as well as interesting trivia from the period I was investigating. While Dr Shahid provided me with important material in the form of books and journals, Mr Khan took me around museums and other significant places that offered me valuable insights into the subject. I am grateful to Dr Shahid and Mr Khan, without whose help and guidance, the book would have floundered and perhaps met with a premature end. Both are repositories of a wealth of information and their help proved to be crucial in the development of the book in several ways.

I also want to extend my gratitude to Dr Mohammed Safiullah, well-known academic and historian, for his endless patience over my numerous phone calls and non-stop badgering. Dr Safiullah's prompt replies, sharing of vital pieces of evidence as well as information and his ever-approachable attitude went a long way in adding value to the text and in providing me with compelling facts and figures. I also want to thank eminent scholar and historian Allama Aijaz Farrukh for being kind enough to spare time out of his busy schedule to meet me and throw light upon some crucial facts and information about the subject.

The book, as you will find, showcases different perspectives about several aspects. This would not have been possible without the help received from Dr P. Jogi Naidu, retired deputy director of the Department of Archaeology and Museums, Government of Telangana, who most kindly shared relevant documents that greatly enriched the text. I would also like to thank Dr Pradeep Kumar, dramatist and retired professor of theatre in the Osmania University who most willingly spared the time to speak with me at length and provided me with information which would have been otherwise difficult to access. Mr Pankaj Sethi was also very helpful and took out time to help me with several contacts and information on the subject.

One of the most interesting parts of writing a book are the field trips. In this case, I deeply appreciate the help rendered by Jameela Nishat, a well-known poet and founder and head of the NGO Shaheen Collective–Shaheen's Women Resource and Welfare Association. She was kind enough to help me out and offered me a fresh perspective to the narrative. She sent three of her team members, Pooja, Zaira and Archana with me on a tour of the old city. The three young girls took me around various sites and painstakingly made notes from several books in libraries, took photographs and spoke to people judiciously on my behalf. A big thank you to all the three girls. It was perhaps one of my most pleasant outings.

Talking of enthusiastic youngsters, I am so thankful to my friend, poet Ramesh Karthik Nayak, winner of the Sahitya Akademi Yuva Puraskar, who not just took the effort to visit me several times and initiated in-depth discussions about Bhagmati's origin, but promptly called up his contacts across the globe at unearthly hours and put me in touch with them for chat sessions on the subject.

Hyderabad perhaps wouldn't have endeared me as much if it weren't for my friends who took me under their wing right from day one and made me so much a part of the city. Heartfelt thanks to my Hyderabadi friends without whose constant cheering and warm hospitality, writing this book would not have been such a pleasant experience. I thank our dear friends, Sravan and Sridevi, who always welcomed us into their beautiful home every time we visited Hyderabad. Their constant encouragement and interest in my book and in checking out facts for me really helped. Our friends, Giridhar and Rekha, always kept their doors open for any untimely visits from me and have gently, over the years, nurtured and nourished my love for the city. My dear friends, Manoj, who as always insisted I write a non-fiction book on the subject and his lovely wife, Renu were instrumental in those early years to help me understand and feel the city's cultural tapestry.

I also extend my warm thanks to our dear friends C.T. Mathew and his wife Jaya, who fed me delicious appam and chicken curry each time I visited Hyderabad and enthusiastically helped me out in whatever way they could. They further introduced me to heritage enthusiast, Gordon Rattansey, who I thank profusely for going out of his way in arranging a meeting for me with a well-known social activist. I also thank my dear friends, Rosabelle and Malcolm Wolfe and their beautiful daughters, Sarah and Tabitha, who have always greeted me with open arms, and even took the trouble of accompanying me during one of my night jaunts to the old city during Ramzan and waited patiently for hours in the middle of the night while I went up to the Charminar and looked up the area.

But my list of Hyderabadi friends will not be complete until I mention Vijay Marur, the person who initiated me into becoming an honorary Hyderabadi. I got my first taste of all things Hyderabadi thanks to him. In fact, he was largely responsible for me falling in love with the city. And above all, like true Hyderabadis, both Vijay, who is unfortunately not amidst us anymore, and his wife Lata embraced me warmly even as I stepped on the soil of Hyderabad and introduced me to the famed hospitality and *tehzeeb* of this city of love. Vijay would have been so happy to see the book!

I would also like to thank my dear childhood friend Shuchi Gupta, who cheerfully sat through various sessions of talks on Hyderabad and Bhagmati and recorded them for me.

I would like to extend my thanks to librarian Thallapelly Sambaiah of the Archaeology Department Museum Library, who brought out from the dusty shelves, volumes of books that helped me enormously in my research.

A huge thank you to my brilliant literary agent Kanishka Gupta who believed in the book more than I did.

I extend my heartfelt appreciation and many thanks to the excellent editorial team at Westland led by Ajitha G.S. who has been my constant support and guide and who trusted me with the complex subject that I hesitatingly undertook; my exceptional editors Kushalrani Gulab, who gave my story its shape and form thus enhancing its readability, and Pallavi Mohan, who ran a fine comb through it, polished and refined it, trimming the rough edges thus improving the text greatly to make it a smooth read. My brainstorming sessions with the editorial team were most exciting and a rather pleasant experience for me. I would also like to thank Westland designer Saurabh Garge for the beautiful cover design.

Last, but not the least, my warm thanks to my husband Rajib, who accompanied me on many Hyderabad visits and city tours and sat through most meetings, offering me valuable insights and advice. I would also like to thank my son Pronoy, whose critical appreciation of the manuscript helped me look into areas that I had missed. I also thank my mother for her constant encouragement and blessings.

Notes

Preface

1. Syed Ali Asgar Bilgrami, *Landmarks of the Deccan: A comprehensive guide to the archaeological remains of the city and suburbs of Hyderabad* (Government Central Press, Hyderabad-Deccan, 1927).

Chapter 1. 450 Years Ago

1. Also called Mathnawi—it's a kind of a poem written in rhyming couplets, closely tied to Islamic theology, philosophy and legends.
2. Masud Husain, *Mohammad Quli Qutb Shah*, trans. Mehr Afshan Farooqi (Sahitya Akademi, Delhi, 1996).
3. *Kulliyat-e-Sultan Mohammad Quli Qutb Shah*, sourced from Masud Husain, *Mohammad Quli Qutb Shah*, trans. Mehr Afshan Farooqi.
4. *Ibid.*
5. Heidi R.M. Pauwels, *Indian Literature and Popular Cinema: Recasting Classics* (Taylor & Francis, United Kingdom, 2007).
6. K.S.R. Murti, 'References to Bhagnagar in the Contemporary Telugu Literature of Qutb Shahi Period, and the Enigma of Bhagmati and Bhagirathi', *Salar Jung Museum*, (XXVII-XXVIII), 1990- 1991.
7. A Persian genre of storytelling in which serialised stories of extensive length are orally narrated in the dastan goi style.

8. Narendra Luther, *Prince, poet, lover, builder: Muhammad Quli Qutb Shah, the founder of Hyderabad* (Publications Division, Ministry of Information & Broadcasting, 2010).
9. Haroon Khan Sherwani, *Muḥammad-Qulī Quṭb Shāh, founder of Haidarabad* (Asia Publishing House, 1967).
10. Ferishta, *Ferishta's History of Dekkan, from the First Mahummedan Conquests,* trans. Jonathan Scott (Cambridge University Press, United Kingdom, 2013).
11. *Kulliyat-e-Sultan Mohammad Quli Qutb Shah,* sourced from Masud Husain, *Mohammad Quli Qutb Shah,* trans. Mehr Afshan Farooqi.
12. *Ibid.*
13. *Ibid.*
14. *Tarekh-e-Qutb Shahi Hyderabad* by Sayyed Burhanuddin Ahmad, sourced from Serish Nanisetti, *Golconda/Bagnagar/Hyderabad: Rise and Fall of a Global Metropolis in Medieval India* (India, 2019).
15. *Kulliyat-e-Sultan Mohammad Quli Qutb Shah,* sourced from Masud Husain, *Mohammad Quli Qutb Shah,* trans. Mehr Afshan Farooqi.
16. *Ibid.*
17. *Ibid.*
18. 'Bhogamwar, an offshoot of the Devadasi caste, was generally associated with music, dance and song. Akbar ordained that they should be called Kalavants.' K.S.R. Murti, 'References to Bhagnagar in the Contemporary Telugu Literature of Qutb Shahi Period, and the Enigma of Bhagmati and Bhagirathi'.
19. Also called manqabat, these are poems written in praise, glory and accomplishments, especially of the prophet and his companions.
20. *Kulliyat-e-Sultan Mohammad Quli Qutb Shah,* sourced from Masud Husain, *Mohammad Quli Qutb Shah,* trans. Mehr Afshan Farooqi.
21. A collection of poems written by one author.
22. Masud Husain, *Mohammad Quli Qutb Shah,* trans. Mehr Afshan Farooqi.

23. T Hyder Reza Zabeth, 'The Role of Iranian Migrant Scholars in the Advancement of Sciences During the Qutb Shahi Period in Dakan', *Imam Reza*. https://www.imamreza.net/old/eng/imamreza.php?id=3885.
24. According to the Merriam-Webster dictionary, it is a pulpit address of prescribed form that is read in mosques on Fridays at noon prayer and contains an acknowledgment of the sovereignty of the reigning prince.
25. William Harrison Moreland, *Relations of Golconda in the early seventeenth century* (Hakluyt Society, United Kingdom, 1931).
26. *Ibid.*
27. *Kulliyat-e-Sultan Mohammad Quli Qutb Shah*, sourced from *Mohammad Quli Qutb Shah*, Masud Husain, *Mohammad Quli Qutb Shah*, trans. Mehr Afshan Farooqi.
28. *Ibid.*
29. *Ibid.*
30. *Ibid.*
31. *Ibid.*
32. *Ibid.*
33. *Ibid.*
34. Masud Husain, *Mohammad Quli Qutb Shah*, trans. Mehr Afshan Farooqi.
35. *Ibid.*
36. Masud Husain, *Mohammad Quli Qutb Shah*, trans. Mehr Afshan Farooqi.
37. *Ibid.*
38. *Ibid.*
39. *Bhagmati* by Makhdoom Mohiuddin, translation sourced from Syeda Imam, *The Untold Charminar* (Penguin Books Limited, India, 2008).

Chapter 2. The Reluctant Kings

1. 'The most powerful of the Kings of the Decan, next to Viziapour, is the King of Golconda.' Surendranath Sen, *Indian travels of Thevenot and Careri* (National Archives of India, New Delhi, 1949).
2. 'We have spoken of the wealth of the Golconda country in jewels and gold. The mines of Golconda are a proverb, but it is as well to state at once that there never was a diamond mine at Golconda, or anywhere within eighty miles of the fort. The celebrated diamond mines were all situated in the country that now forms the British districts of Kurnul, Cuddapah, and Nellore, and the diamonds were brought to, and stored in, the royal fort of Golconda, but as the merchants mostly re-sorted there, they gave the name of Golconda diamonds to stones that were really found elsewhere.' James Dunning Baker Gribble, *A History of the Deccan* (Luzac and Company, United Kingdom, 1896).
3. 'His military genius combined with the noble urge of a Shia zealot acted as a powerful impetus for the extension of his domain.' Tukaram Nagesh Devare, *A Short History of Persian Literature: At the Bahmanī, the 'Ādilshāhī and the Qutbshāhī Courts–Deccan* (Routledge, 2018).
4. 'There is no epitaph on Jamshed's grave and other than some doubtful coins in which Jamshed is spelt as Janbshid, no coin of Jamshed is found anywhere else.' Haroon Khan Sherwani, *Muḥammad-Qulī Quṭb Shāh, founder of Haidarabad.*
5. 'It is doubtful whether the coins attributed to Jamshid and Subhan are genuine.' H.K. Sherwani and P.M. Joshi, *History of Medieval Deccan, 1295-1724* (Government of Andhra Pradesh, 1974).
6. Tukaram Nagesh Devare, *A Short History of Persian Literature: At the Bahmanī, the 'Ādilshāhī and the Qutbshāhī Courts–Deccan.*
7. 'He gave himself up to the pleasures of the table and eventually sank into gross debauchery, possibly to deaden the pain of affliction. He

was a man of violent passions at the best of times, and his fearful malady so inflamed his temper that at its close his reign was really a reign of terror. Many paid the maximum penalty for the most trivial offences.' Sha Rocco, *A Guide to Golconda Fort and Tombs* (Government Central Press, Hyderabad-Deccan, 1946).

8. Mandana Mangeli, 'Persian Literature and Culture of the Qutb Shahi and the Safavid Periods: A Comparative Study.' Jawaharlal Nehru University (2012), http://hdl.handle.net/10603/119868.
9. Vedagiri Rambabu, *The Story of a Great City*, trans. Sai Prasad Alahari (1991).
10. 'In his foreign policy, he always tried to steer a middle course, and rarely did he attempt to extend his dominion beyond the region where Telugu was spoken as the mother tongue.' Haroon Khan Sherwani, *Muḥammad-Qulī Quṭb Shāh, founder of Haidarabad*.
11. M. Rama Rao, *Glimpses of Dakkan History* (Orient Longmans, India, 1951).
12. 'Throughout the rest of the Golconda history, we find the Sultans more engaged with their own affairs and abstaining—comparatively speaking—from interfering in the constant disputes between Bijapur and Ahmednagar. It was almost as though they were reluctant kings.' James Dunning Baker Gribble, *A History of the Deccan*.
13. Vedagiri Rambabu, *The Story of a Great City*, trans. Sai Prasad Alahari.
14. 'The long reign of Ibrahim Qutb Shah (1550-1580) may be said to form a high water-mark in the history of the Qutb Shahi kingdom both in the cultural and political spheres. It showed literary flurorescence brought about by the patronage given to Telugu as well as Persian, and the slow but sure rise of the Dakhni idiom which later flowed into Urdu.' Haroon Khan Sherwani, *Muḥammad-Qulī Quṭb Shāh, founder of Haidarabad*.
15. Haroon Khan Sherwani, *Muḥammad-Qulī Quṭb Shāh, founder of Haidarabad*.

16. 'Ibrahim believed that the boy was destined to be great and celebrated his birth with lot of enthusiasm.' Vedagiri Rambabu, *The Story of a Great City*, trans. Sai Prasad Alahari.
17. *Ibid.*
18. K.S.R. Murti, 'References to Bhagnagar in the Contemporary Telugu Literature of Qutb Shahi Period, and the Enigma of Bhagmati and Bhagirathi'.
19. Laura Weinstein, 'Variations on a Persian Theme: The Dīwān of Muhammad Quli Qutb Shah and the Birth of the Illustrated Urdu Dīwān', *The Visual World of Muslim India: The Art, Culture and Society of the Deccan in the Early Modern Era*, 2014, pp. 179-204.
20. Carla Petievich, 'The Feminine and Cultural Syncretism in Early Dakani Poetry', *Annual of Urdu Studies*, 8, 1993 sourced from Laura Weinstein, 'Variations on a Persian Theme: The Dīwān of Muhammad Quli Qutb Shah and the Birth of the Illustrated Urdu Dīwān'.
21. *Kulliyat-e-Sultan Mohammad Quli Qutb Shah*, sourced from Masud Husain, *Mohammad Quli Qutb Shah*, trans. Mehr Afshan Farooqi.
22. *Ibid.*
23. *Ibid.*
24. *Ibid.*
25. Surendranath Sen, *Indian travels of Thevenot and Careri*.

Chapter 3. Bhagmati's Bhagyanagar or Ali's Hyderabad?

1. Ameer Ahmad Khusro, *Shahr-e-Nigaran* sourced from *https://www.rekhta.org/nazms/shahr-e-nigaaraan-hyderabad-jise-shahr-e-nigaaraan-kahiye-ameer-ahmad-khusro-nazms*.
2. *Tuzuke-Qutbshahi* quoted in Syed Ali Asgar Bilgrami, *Landmarks of the Deccan: A comprehensive guide to the archaeological remains of the city and suburbs of Hyderabad*.

3. Anand Raj Varma, *Hyderabad: Mohalley, Gali aur Kunche* (Om Publications, 2015).
4. Jean-Baptiste Tavernier and Valentine Ball, *Travels in India: By Jean-Baptiste Tavernier* (Macmillan and Company, United Kingdom, 1889).
5. Mahomed Kasim Ferishta, *History of the Rise of the Mahomedan Power in India, Till the Year AD 1612. Vol III.*, trans. John Briggs (Longman, Rees, Orme, Brown, and Green, United Kingdom, 1829).
6. The Musi was known as the Nerva during the Qutb Shahi period and later came to be called Musi after Moses.
7. Surendranath Sen, *Indian travels of Thevenot and Careri.*
8. Ian Austin, *City of Legends: The Story of Hyderabad* (Penguin, India, 1992).
9. Syed Ali Asgar Bilgrami, *Landmarks of the Deccan: A comprehensive guide to the archaeological remains of the city and suburbs of Hyderabad.*
10. A gold coin equivalent of four and a half Mughal rupees.
11. Dharmendra Prasad, *Social and Cultural Geography of Hyderabad City: A Historical Perspective* (Inter-India Publications, India, 1986).
12. Surendranath Sen, *Indian travels of Thevenot and Careri.*
13. M.A. Nayeem, *The Heritage of the Qutb Shahis of Golconda and Hyderabad* (Hyderabad Publishers, India, 2006).
14. Jean-Baptiste Tavernier and Valentine Ball, *Travels in India: By Jean-Baptiste Tavernier.*
15. Surendranath Sen, *Indian travels of Thevenot and Careri.*
16. Anand Raj Varma, *Hyderabad: Mohalley, Gali aur Kunche.*
17. Syed Ali Asgar Bilgrami, *Landmarks of the Deccan: A comprehensive guide to the archaeological remains of the city and suburbs of Hyderabad.*

18. Surendranath Sen, *Indian travels of Thevenot and Careri.*
19. 'Having adjusted my measures, I found that Bagnagar was five thousand six hundred and fifty Paces in length, to wit, two thousand four hundred and fifty from the Bridge to the Towers, and from thence, through the Meidan to the Gate which leads to Masulipatan, three thousand two hundred Paces.' Surendranath Sen, *Indian travels of Thevenot and Careri.*
20. Jadunath Sarkar, *A Short History of Aurangzib* (Orient BlackSwan, India, 2009).
21. *Ibid.*
22. Richard M. Eaton, *A Social History of the Deccan, 1300-1761: Eight Indian Lives* (Cambridge University Press, United Kingdom, 2005.
23. Laura M. Leming, 'Sociological Explorations: What is Religious Agency?', *The Sociological Quarterly*, 48(1), 2007, pp. 73-92.
24. Syed Ali Asgar Bilgrami, *Landmarks of the Deccan: A comprehensive guide to the archaeological remains of the city and suburbs of Hyderabad.*
25. Richard M. Eaton and Phillip B. Wagoner. *Power, memory, architecture: Contested sites on India's Deccan Plateau, 1300-1600* (Oxford University Press, 2013).
26. M.A. Qaiyum, noted archaeologist and ex-deputy director of Department of Archaeology and Museums.
27. An alam is processional standard topped by a finial.
28. Dharmendra Prasad, *Social and Cultural Geography of Hyderabad City: A Historical Perspective.*
29. Syed Ali Asgar Bilgrami, *Landmarks of the Deccan: A comprehensive guide to the archaeological remains of the city and suburbs of Hyderabad.*
30. *Ibid.*
31. Surendranath Sen, *Indian travels of Thevenot and Careri.*

32. Aurangzeb came pounding at the doors of Golconda thrice during the Qutb Shahi reign—once during Abdullah's reign and twice during Abul Hasan's reign.
33. K.S.R. Murti, 'References to Bhagnagar in the Contemporary Telugu Literature of Qutb Shahi Period, and the Enigma of Bhagmati and Bhagirathi'.
34. *Ibid.*
35. Yogesh Sharma, 'From Pondicherry to Surat: The travels of Francois Martin', *India International Centre Quarterly*, 30(3/4), 2003, pp. 122-136.
36. 'History of Abu al-Fath Sultan Muhammad Kuli Kutb Shah, who built Bhagnagar or Haidarabdd, and transferred his capital from Gulkundah to the newly-erected city, to his death in A.H. 1020 (1611).' William Hook Morley, *A Descriptive Catalogue of the Historical Manuscripts in the Arabic and Persian Languages Preserved in the Library of The Royal Asiatic Society of Great Britain and Ireland* (Parker and Son, United Kingdom, 1854).
37. Serish Nanisetti, *Golconda/Bagnagar/Hyderabad: Rise and Fall of a Global Metropolis in Medieval India.*
38. Richard Burn and Charles Fawcett, *The Travels of the Abbé Carré in India and the Near East, 1672 to 1674*, trans. Lady Fawcett (Asian Educational Services, Delhi/Madras, 1990).
39. S. Umamaheshwar, 'Bhagnagar, Bhagyanagar or Hyderabad', *Academia. https://www.academia.edu/96249095/BHAGNAGAR_BHAGYANAGAR_OR_HYDERABAD.*
40. *Ibid.*
41. *Ibid.*
42. *Ibid.*
43. *Ibid.*
44. *Ibid.*
45. *Ibid.*

46. *Ibid.*
47. *Ibid.*

Chapter 4. Whispering Graves

1. Serish Nanisetti, *Golconda/Bagnagar/Hyderabad: Rise and Fall of a Global Metropolis in Medieval India*, p. 218.
2. William Foster, *Early travels in India, 1583-1619* (Oxford University Press, London, 1921). Foster wrote this in 1921, clarifying that Finch meant 'Bhagnagar, the original name of the city of Hyderabad'.
3. Gita Dharampal, 'Heinrich von Poser's travelogue to the Deccan', *Quarterly Journal of the Mythic Society*, 73, 1982, p. 108.
4. Narendra Luther, 'On the Historicity of Bhagmati', *Salar Jung Museum Bi-Annual Research Journal*, Vol. XXIX-XXX, 1992-93. https://salarjungmuseum.in/images/publications/publication6.pdf.
5. S. Umamaheshwar, 'Bhagnagar, Bhagyanagar or Hyderabad'.
6. M.A. Nayeem, *The Heritage of the Qutb Shahis of Golconda and Hyderabad*.
7. K.S.R. Murti, 'References to Bhagnagar in the Contemporary Telugu Literature of Qutb Shahi Period, and the Enigma of Bhagmati and Bhagirathi'.
8. Narendra Luther, *Prince, poet, lover, builder: Muhammad Quli Qutb Shah, the founder of Hyderabad*.
9. Mir Ayoob Ali Khan, 'For Hyderabadis, Bhagmati is Vital Part of History,' *The Times of India*, 22 March 2010, https://timesofindia.indiatimes.com/city/hyderabad/for-hyderabadis-bhagmati-is-vital-part-of-history/articleshow/5709733.cms.
10. *Kulliyat-e-Sultan Mohammad Quli Qutb Shah*, sourced from Masud Husain, *Mohammad Quli Qutb Shah*, trans. Mehr Afshan Farooqi.
11. *Ibid.*

12. 'The air of Golconda AD 1586 not agreeing with his conftitution, he founded a city at about eight miles diftance, which he called Bhaugnuggur, after his miftrefs Bhaug, a celebrated courtesan.' Ferishta, *Ferishta's History of Dekkan, from the First Mahummedan Conquests*, trans. Jonathan Scott.
13. *Kulliyat-e-Sultan Mohammad Quli Qutb Shah*, sourced from Masud Husain, *Mohammad Quli Qutb Shah*, trans. Mehr Afshan Farooqi.

Chapter 5. Hyderabad – An Ode to Love

1. Ian Austin, *City of Legends: The Story of Hyderabad.*
2. Narendra Luther, *Legend[o]tes of Hyderabad* (Niyogi Books, India, 2014; Dharmendra Prasad, *Social and Cultural Geography of Hyderabad City: A Historical Perspective.*
3. Karen Leonard, 'Indo-Muslim Culture in Hyderabad: Old City Neighborhoods in the 19th Century.' in *Indo-Muslim Cultures in Transition*, (Brill, 2012), pp. 165-188.
4. Karen Leonard, 'Hyderabad: Continuities and Transformations.' *Urban Life: Readings in the Anthropology of the City* 351 (2018).
5. K.S.S. Seshan, *Hyderabad-400: Saga of a City* (Association of British Council Scholars, Andhra Pradesh Chapter, India, 1993).
6. Narendra Luther, *Prince, poet, lover, builder: Muhammad Quli Qutb Shah, the founder of Hyderabad.*
7. *Ibid.*
8. Richard M. Eaton, *A Social History of the Deccan, 1300-1761: Eight Indian Lives.*
9. Ian Austin, *City of Legends: The Story of Hyderabad.*
10. Pushkar Sohoni, 'The Hunt for a Location.' *Asian ethnology* 77(1/2) (2018), pp. 215-234.
11. Vinita Pandey, 'Changing Facets of Hyderabadi Tehzeeb: Are we missing anything?' *Space and Culture, India* 3(1) (2015), pp. 17-29.
12. Anand Raj Varma, *Hyderabad: Mohalley, Gali aur Kunche.*

Bibliography

Books

- 'Muntakhab-al Lubab of Muhammad Hashim, Khafi Khan' in Henry Miers Elliot, *The History of India, as Told by Its Own Historians: The Muhammadan period: Ed. from the Posthumous Papers of the Late Sir H. M. Elliot*, ed. John Dowson (Trübner & Co, London, 1867).
- Alpana Pandey, *Medieval Andhra: A Socio-Historical Perspective* (Partridge Publishing India, United Kingdom, 2015).
- Anand Raj Varma, *Hyderabad: Mohalley, Gali aur Kunche* (Om Publications, 2015).
- 'Azīz Aḥmad, *An Intellectual History of Islam in India* (Edinburgh U.P., Germany, 1969).
- Dharmendra Prasad, *Social and Cultural Geography of Hyderabad City: A Historical Perspective* (Inter-India Publications, India, 1986).
- Dr Rahimuddin Kemal, *Romance of Kings and Commoners in Golcunda* (Fase Brothers, Hyderabad).
- Edgar Thurston and K. Rangachari, *Castes and Tribes of Southern India* (Asian Educational Services, New Delhi, 2001).
- Ferishta, *Ferishta's History of Dekkan, from the First Mahummedan Conquests,* trans. Jonathan Scott (Cambridge University Press, United Kingdom, 2013).

- Francis Steingass, *A Comprehensive Persian-English Dictionary: Including the Arabic Words and Phrases to be Met with in Persian Literature, Being, Johnson and Richardson's Persian, Arabic, and English Dictionary, Revised, Enlarged, and Entirely Reconstructed* (Asian Educational Services, India, 1992).
- Gita Dharampal, 'Heinrich von Poser's travelogue to the Deccan', *Quarterly Journal of the Mythic Society*, 73, 1982.
- Ghulam Yazdani, *Antiquities of Bidar* (Baptist Mission Press, Calcutta, 1917).
- Gijs Kruijtzer, *Xenophobia in Seventeenth-Century India* (Leiden University Press, Leiden, 2009).
- H.K. Sherwani and P.M. Joshi, *History of Medieval Deccan, 1295-1724* (Government of Andhra Pradesh, 1974).
- Haroon Khan Sherwani, *Cultural Trends in Medieval India: Architecture, Painting, Literature & Language* (Asia Publishing House, India, 1968).
- Haroon Khan Sherwani, *Muḥammad-Qulī Quṭb Shāh, founder of Haidarabad.* (Asia Publishing House, 1967).
- Heidi R.M. Pauwels, *Indian Literature and Popular Cinema: Recasting Classics* (Taylor & Francis, United Kingdom, 2007).
- Ian Austin, *City of Legends: The Story of Hyderabad* (Penguin, India, 1992).
- Ishrat Jahan, *Socio-Cultural Life in Medieval History* (Laxmi Book Publication, Solapur, 2018).
- Jadunath Sarkar, *A Short History of Aurangzib* (Orient BlackSwan, India, 2009).
- James Dunning Baker Gribble, *A History of the Deccan* (Luzac and Company, United Kingdom, 1896).
- Jean-Baptiste Tavernier and Valentine Ball, *Travels in India: By Jean-Baptiste Tavernier* (Macmillan and Company, United Kingdom, 1889).

- K.S.S. Seshan, *Hyderabad-400: Saga of a City* (Association of British Council Scholars, Andhra Pradesh Chapter, India, 1993).
- Kavita Datla, *The Language of Secular Islam: Urdu Nationalism and Colonial India* (University of Hawaii Press, Germany, 2013).
- Kousar J. Azam, *Languages and Literary Cultures in Hyderabad* (Taylor & Francis, United Kingdom, 2017).
- Laura E. Parodi, *The Visual World of Muslim India: The Art, Culture and Society of the Deccan in the Early Modern Era* (Bloomsbury, 2022).
- M. Rama Rao, *Glimpses of Dakkan History* (Orient Longmans, India, 1951).
- M.A. Nayeem, *The Heritage of the Qutb Shahis of Golconda and Hyderabad* (Hyderabad Publishers, India, 2006).
- Mahomed Kasim Ferishta, *History of the Rise of the Mahomedan Power in India, Till the Year AD 1612. Vol III.*, trans. John Briggs (Longman, Rees, Orme, Brown, and Green, United Kingdom, 1829).
- Masud Husain, *Mohammad Quli Qutb Shah*, trans. Mehr Afshan Farooqi (Sahitya Akademi, Delhi, 1996).
- Mohibbul Hasan, *Historians of Medieval India* (Aakar, India, 2018).
- Nagendra Kumar Singh, *Global Encyclopaedia of the South Indian Dalit's Ethnography* (Global Vision Publishing House, New Delhi, 2006).
- Narendra Luther, *Prince, poet, lover, builder: Muhammad Quli Qutb Shah, the founder of Hyderabad* (Publications Division, Ministry of Information & Broadcasting, 2010).
- Narendra Luther, *Hyderabad: A Biography* (Oxford University Press, India, 2006).

- Narendra Luther, *Legend[o]tes of Hyderabad* (Niyogi Books, India, 2014).
- Ram Babu Saksena, *A History of Urdu Literature* (R. N. Lal, India, 1940).
- Raza Alikhan, *Hyderabad 400 Years 1591-1991* (India).
- Richard Burn and Charles Fawcett, *The Travels of the Abbé Carré in India and the Near East, 1672 to 1674*, trans. Lady Fawcett (Asian Educational Services, Delhi/Madras, 1990).
- Richard Henry Major, *India in the fifteenth century: being a collection of narratives of voyages to India* (Hakluyt Society, London, 1974).
- Richard M. Eaton, *A Social History of the Deccan, 1300-1761: Eight Indian Lives* (Cambridge University Press, United Kingdom, 2005).
- Richard M. Eaton and Phillip B. Wagoner. *Power, memory, architecture: Contested sites on India's Deccan Plateau, 1300-1600* (Oxford University Press, 2013).
- Samuel Purchas, *Purchas His Pilgrimage: Or, a Relations of the World and the Religions Observed in All Ages and Places Discovered, from the Creation Unto This Present* (Fetherstone, London, 1613).
- Serish Nanisetti, *Golconda/Bagnagar/Hyderabad: Rise and Fall of a Global Metropolis in Medieval India* (India, 2019).
- Sha Rocco, *A Guide to Golconda Fort and Tombs* (Government Central Press, Hyderabad-Deccan, 1946).
- Sha Rocco, *Golconda and the Qutb Shahs* (Government Central Press, Hyderabad-Deccan, 1929).
- Siddiqi, Abdul Majeed, *History of Golcunda* (Literary Publications, India, 1956).
- Sita Anantha Raman, *Women in India: A Social and Cultural History* (ABC-CLIO, United States, 2009).

- Srinivas Reddy, *Raya: Krishnadevaraya of Vijayanagara* (Juggernaut, India, 2020).
- Surendranath Sen, *Indian travels of Thevenot and Careri* (National Archives of India, New Delhi, 1949).
- Syed Ali Asgar Bilgrami, *Landmarks of the Deccan:. a comprehensive guide to the archaeological remains of the city and suburbs of Hyderabad* (Government Central Press, Hyderabad-Deccan, 1927).
- Syeda Imam, *The Untold Charminar* (Penguin Books Limited, India, 2008).
- Tukaram Nagesh Devare, *A Short History of Persian Literature: At the Bahmanī, the 'Ādilshāhī and the Qutbshāhī Courts–Deccan* (Routledge, 2018).
- Vedagiri Rambabu, *The Story of a Great City*, trans. Sai Prasad Alahari (1991).
- William Foster, *Early travels in India, 1583-1619* (Oxford University Press, London, 1921).
- William Foster, *The English Factories in India 1618-1669* (Clarendon Press, United Kingdom, 1908).
- William Harrison Moreland, *Relations of Golconda in the early seventeenth century* (Hakluyt Society, United Kingdom, 1931).
- William Hook Morley, *A Descriptive Catalogue of the Historical Manuscripts in the Arabic and Persian Languages Preserved in the Library of The Royal Asiatic Society of Great Britain and Ireland* (Parker and Son, United Kingdom, 1854).

Journals, periodicals and research papers

- 'Absorbing Love Story of Rani Bhagmati Who Married the Sultan of Golconda', *Navrang India*, 16 November 2016, https://www.navrangindia.in/2016/11/absorbing-love-story-of-rani-bhagmati.html.

- 'Communal Riots in Hyderabad: Understanding the Causes', *Economic and Political Weekly,* 45(17), 2010, pp. 14–17. http://www.jstor.org/stable/25664375.
- 'The Many Arts of the Deccan: Nauras', *Asian Art,* 5 March 2015. https://asianartnewspaper.com/nauras-the-many-arts-of-the-deccan/.
- 'Vice President Delivers the First Mohammad Quli Qutub Shah Memorial Lecture', *Press Information Bureau,* 13 April 2017. https://pib.gov.in/PressReleaseIframePage.aspx?PRID=1487830.
- Aafiya Ayman Baseer, 'Is "Puranapul Darwaza"—a Symbol of "Ganga-Jamuni Culture" Losing Sheen In Hyderabad?', *Hyderabad News,* 10 March 2020. https://hydnews.net/2020/03/is-puranapul-darwaza-a-symbol-of-ganga-jamuni-culture-losing-sheen-in-hyderabad/.
- Adarsh, '"Hyderabad Was Never Bhagyanagar". Let's Dismatle This Lie Of Fake Historians', *Kreatley,* 4 December 2021. https://kreately.in/hyderabad/.
- Ameer Ahmad Khusro, *Shahr-e-Nigaran,* https://www.rekhta.org/nazms/shahr-e-nigaaraan-hyderabad-jise-shahr-e-nigaaraan-kahiye-ameer-ahmad-khusro-nazms.
- Arthur L. Campa, 'Folklore and History', *Western Folklore,* 24(1), 1965, pp. 1–5. https://doi.org/10.2307/1498853.
- Aruna Ravikumar, 'Have You Seen The Musi Flow?', *The Hans India,* 25 February 2018. https://www.thehansindia.com/posts/index/Sunday-Hans/2018-02-25/Have-you-seen-the-Musi-flow/361447.
- Benjamin Cohen, 'Modernising the Urban Environment: The Musi River Flood of 1908 in Hyderabad, India', *Environment and History,* 17(3), 2011, pp. 409-432.
- Brandice Palmer, 'Seeking story: Finding the Modern Day Folktale in the Daily News', PhD diss., *University of South Florida,* 2005.

- C.R. Gowri Shanker, 'Bhagmati is Fiction and Not Fact: Experts', *Deccan Chronicle,* 11 September 2016. https://www.deccanchronicle.com/nation/current-affairs/110916/bhagmati-is-fiction-and-not-fact-experts.html.
- Carla Petievich, 'The Feminine and Cultural Syncretism in Early Dakani Poetry', *Annual of Urdu Studies,* 8, 1993.
- Dr Rahul Shastri, 'Bhagyanagar, The people's Hyderabad That Refuses to Die', *Swarajya,* 25 November 2018. https://swarajyamag.com/culture/bhagyanagar-the-peoples-hyderabad-that-refuses-to-die#:~:text=Although%20much%20suppressed%20over%20centuries,Hyderabad%20that%20refuses%20to%20die.
- Edwin Binney, 'Indian Paintings from the Deccan', *Journal of the Royal Society of Arts,* 127(5280), 1979, pp. 784-804.
- Emanuel Bowen, 'A Map of India on the West Side of the Ganges Comprehending the Coasts of Malabar, Cormandel (Sic) and the Island Ceylon, Mid 18th Century'. https://www.grosvenorgallery.com/exhibitions/237/works/artworks-3446-emanuel-bowen-a-map-of-india-on-the-west-side-mid-18th-century/.
- Fareeda Begum, 'Language and Literature During Deccan Sultanates', *Gulbarga University,* 2017. http://hdl.handle.net/10603/143136.
- Fatima Maryam, 'Relations of the Sufis with the rulers of Deccan 14th-17th centuries', *Aligarh Muslim University,* (2012). https://core.ac.uk/download/pdf/144526781.pdf.
- Hyder Reza Zabeth, 'The Role of Iranian Migrant Scholars in the Advancement of Sciences During the Qutb Shahi Period in Dakan', *Imam Reza. https://www.imamreza.net/old/eng/imamreza.php?id=3885.*
- IANS, 'Hyderabad's Founder Quli Qutb Shah Was Secular Ruler', *Business Standard,* 13 April 2017. https://www.business-

standard.com/article/news-ians/hyderabad-s-founder-quli-qutub-shah-was-secular-ruler-117041300897_1.html.

- 'Interface of History & Fiction in Urban Legends: Told & Untold Stories of Hyderabad', presented at the International Conference on 'Cities in Indian History', *University of Hyderabad,* 16-17 December 2014.
- J.S. Ifthekhar, Did Bhagmati Really Exist?', *The Hindu,* 16 November 2021. https://www.thehindu.com/news/cities/Hyderabad/did-bhagmati-really-exist/article5339909.ece.
- K.S.R. Murti, 'References to Bhagnagar in the Contemporary Telugu Literature of Qutb Shahi Period, and the Enigma of Bhagmati and Bhagirathi', *Salar Jung Museum,* (XXVII-XXVIII) (1990-1991).
- Kamal K. Misra and K. Koteswara Rao, 'Theogamy in Rural India: Socio-Cultural Dimensions of the "Jogini" System in Andhra Pradesh', *Indian Anthropologist,* 32(1/2), 2002, pp. 1-24.
- Karen Leonard, 'Courtesans of Hyderabad and Beyond: Claiming Significance', in Karen Leonard, *Hyderabad and Hyderabadis* (Manohar Publishers & Distributors, New Delhi, 2013).
- Karen Leonard, 'Hyderabad: Continuities and Transformations', *Urban Life: Readings in the Anthropology of the City,* 351, 2018.
- Karen Leonard, 'Indo-Muslim Culture in Hyderabad: Old City Neighborhoods in the 19th Century' in *Indo-Muslim Cultures in Transition,* 2012, pp. 165-188.
- Karen Leonard, 'The Deccani Synthesis in Old Hyderabad. An Historiographic Essay', *Journal of the Pakistan Historical Society,* 21(4), 1973, p. 205.
- Karen Leonard, 'The Hyderabad Political System and its Participants', *The Journal of Asian Studies,* 30(3), 1971, pp. 569-582.

- Karen Ruffle, 'Making Shiʿism an Indian Religion: A Perspective from the Qutb Shahi Deccan', *ReOrient*, 5(2), 2020, pp. 287-304.
- Laura M. Leming, 'Sociological Explorations: What is Religious Agency?', *The Sociological Quarterly*, 48(1) 2007, pp. 73-92.
- Laura Weinstein, 'Variations on a Persian Theme: The Dīwān of Muhammad Quli Qutb Shah and the Birth of the Illustrated Urdu Dīwān', *The Visual World of Muslim India: The Art, Culture and Society of the Deccan in the Early Modern Era*, 2014, pp. 179-204.
- Lavanya, B, 'Representation of women in the miniature paintings in the Deccan school', PhD diss., *University of Hyderabad*, 30 May 2004.
- Linda Joy Epp, '"Violating The Sacred"? The Social Reform of Devadasis Among Dalits in Karnataka, India', *York University*, 1997. https://www.collectionscanada.gc.ca/obj/s4/f2/dsk2/ftp03/NQ27290.pdf.
- Mandana Mangeli, 'Persian Literature and Culture of the Qutb Shahi and the Safavid Periods: A Comparative Study', *Jawaharlal Nehru University*, 2012. http://hdl.handle.net/10603/119868.
- Maqubool, 'Agriculture and irrigation system under Qutb Shahi period', *Osmania University*, 2014. http://hdl.handle.net/10603/27431.
- Marika Sardar, 'Golconda through time: A mirror of the evolving Deccan', PhD diss., *New York University*, 2007.
- Marika Sardar, 'The Early Foundations of Golconda and the Rise of Fortifications in the Fourteenth-Century Deccan', *South Asian Studies*, 27(1), 2011, pp. 25-50.
- Mir Ayoob Ali Khan, 'For Hyderabadis, Bhagmati is Vital Part of History', *The Times of India*, 22 March 2010. https://timesofindia.indiatimes.com/city/hyderabad/for-hyderabadis-bhagmati-is-vital-part-of-history/articleshow/5709733.cms.

- Mohan Guruswamy, 'Celebrating a Long Gone Hyderabad', *National Herald*, 4 April 2018. https://www.nationalheraldindia.com/india/celebrating-a-long-gone-hyderabad-on-453-foundation-day-anniversary.
- Mohan Guruswamy, 'Now 5 Acres for Charminar in Hyderabad? 'Conflict' around Bhagyalaxmi Temple', *Counterview*, 21 November 2019. https://www.counterview.net/2019/11/now-5-acres-for-charminar-in-hyderabad.html.
- Narendra Luther, 'On the Historicity of Bhagmati', *Salar Jung Museum Bi-Annual Research Journal*, Vol. XXIX-XXX, 1992-93. https://salarjungmuseum.in/images/publications/publication6.pdf.
- Pushkar Sohoni, 'The Hunt for a Location', *Asian ethnology*, 77(1/2), 2018, pp. 215-234.
- Pushkar Sohoni, 'The non-issue of coinage: The monetary policies of the post-Bahmani sultanates', *Journal of the Royal Asiatic Society*, 28(4), 2018, pp. 645-659.
- Rahul Shastri & Samvit Kendra, 'Bhāgyanagar—The Living Root of Hyderabad', 2020, https://10.13140/RG.2.2.22172.31369.
- Rayaprolu Swarupa Rani, 'Women, Social change and politics in early 20th century Telangana', PhD diss., *University of Hyderabad*, 1996. https://dspace.uohyd.ac.in/server/api/core/bitstreams/e61dd960-c636-47e7-849c-f3401fb22aee/content.
- Rekha Pande, 'Writing the history of women in the margins: The Courtesans in India', *Mizoram University Journal of Humanities and Social Sciences*, 2018, pp. 1-24.
- Rishika Sadam, 'Bhagyanagar & Bhagyalakshmi—A 16th-Century Tale that's Found Focus in Hyderabad's 2020 Poll', *The Print*, 1 December 2020. https://theprint.in/politics/bhagyanagar-bhagyalakshmi-a-16th-century-tale-thats-found-focus-in-hyderabads-2020-poll/555130/.

- Robert Alan Simpkins, 'Inferring Road Networks and Socio-Political Change through Elite Monuments of the Golconda Kingdom', *South Asian Studies*, 36(1), 2020, pp. 1-19.
- S. Umamaheshwar, 'Bhagnagar, Bhagyanagar or Hyderabad', *Academia, https://www.academia.edu/96249095/BHAGNAGAR_BHAGYANAGAR_OR_HYDERABAD.*
- Saima Afreen, 'Of Finding Bhagmati in History', *The New Indian Express,* 27 February 2020. https://www.newindianexpress.com/hyderabad/2020/Feb/26/of-finding-bhagmati-in-history-2108977.html.
- Sanjay Subrahmanyam, 'Persians, pilgrims and Portuguese: The travails of Masulipatnam shipping in the western Indian Ocean, 1590–1665', *Modern Asian Studies,* 22(3), 1988, pp. 503-530.
- Shaik Ahmed Ali, 'Our First School,' *The Times of India,* 3 October 2001.
- https://timesofindia.indiatimes.com/our-first-school/articleshow/922730338.cms.
- Simon Charsley, 'Madiga and Dalit: exploring the heritage', *NFSC Books and Monographs,* 2009.
- Sumit Guha, 'Transitions and Translations: Regional Power and Vernacular Identity in the Dakhan, 1500-1800', *Comparative Studies of South Asia, Africa and the Middle East,* 24(2), 2004, pp. 23-31.
- Surabhi Shaurya, 'Hyderabad to Be Renamed Bhagyanagar? Here's How the Name Originates', *India.com,* 4 July 2022.
- https://www.india.com/telangana/hyderabad-to-be-renamed-bhagyanagar-heres-how-the-name-originates-5491204/.
- Syed Akbar, 'From Deluge Misery To Municipal Dump Yard', *The Times of India,* 28 September 2017. https://timesofindia.

indiatimes.com/city/hyderabad/from-deluge-misery-to-municipal-dump-yard/articleshow/60865287.cms.

- Syed Mohammed, 'Fabled Bridge over Musi Stands Ravages of Time', *The Times of India*, 25 July 2017. https://timesofindia.indiatimes.com/city/hyderabad/fabled-bridge-over-musi-stands-ravages-of-time/articleshow/59750274.cms.
- T.S. Sudhir, 'The Birth of Hyderabad and How Charminar Survived the Might of Aurangzeb', *The News Minute*, 29 September 2016. https://www.thenewsminute.com/telangana/birth-hyderabad-and-how-charminar-survived-might-aurangzeb-50594.
- Tahseen Bilgrami, 'Socio Religio Culture During Qutb Shahs.' *Learning Community-An International Journal of Educational and Social Development*, 7(1), 2016, pp. 71-76.
- TNN, 'Legend of Bhagmati is the Monument's Raison D'etre', *The Times of India*, 25 October 2001. https://timesofindia.indiatimes.com/city/hyderabad/legend-of-bhagmati-is-the-monuments-raison-detre/articleshow/2009173575.cms
- Vinita Pandey, 'Changing Facets of Hyderabadi Tehzeeb: Are we missing anything?', *Space and Culture, India*, 3(1), 2015, pp. 17-29.
- Yogesh Sharma, 'From Pondicherry to Surat: the travels of Francois Martin', *India International Centre Quarterly*, 30(3/4), 2003, pp. 122-136.
- Yunus Lasania, 'Hyderabad: Why Any Modernisation Project at Charminar Will Fail,' *The Siasat Daily*, 25 October 2023. https://www.siasat.com/hyderabad-why-any-modernisation-project-at-charminar-will-fail-2456973/
- Yunus Y. Lasania, 'BJP's Push to rename Hyderabad: Does 'Bhagyanagar' Stand a Chance?' *The Wire*, 3 December 2020.
- https://thewire.in/history/hyderabad-bhagyanagar-bjp-push-further-renaming-project